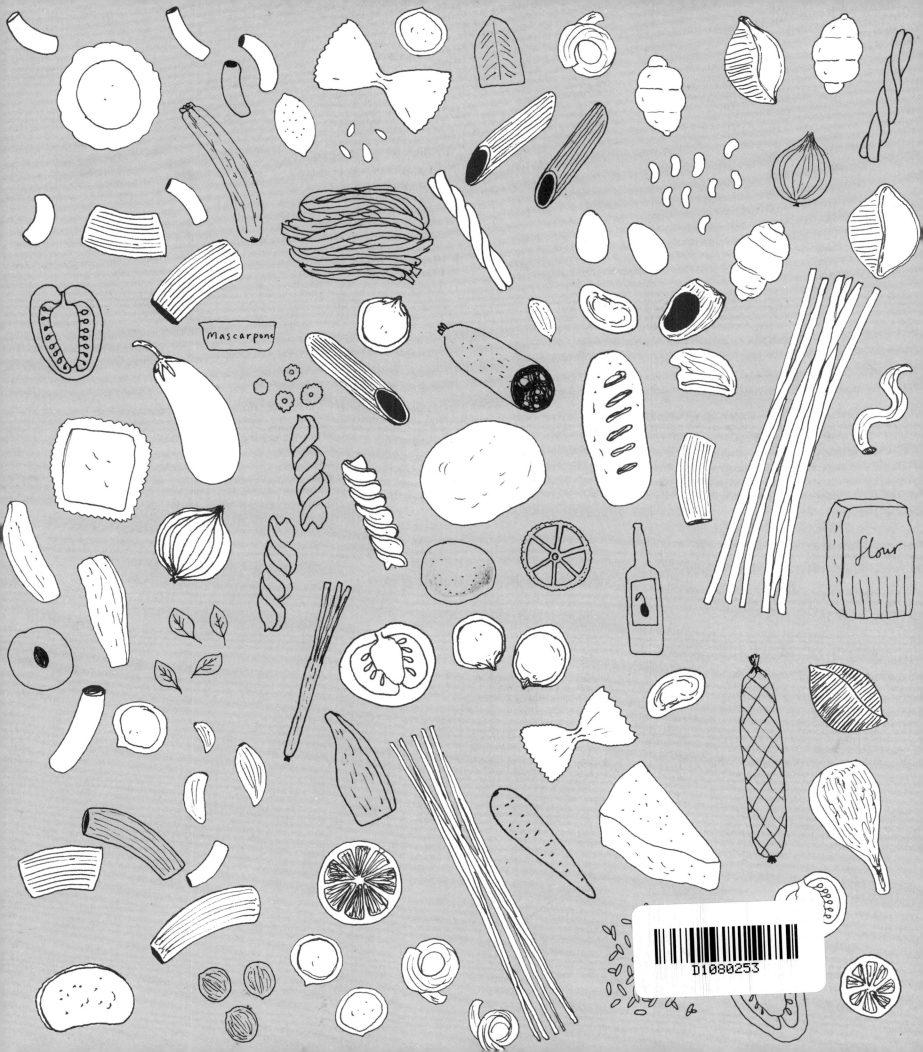

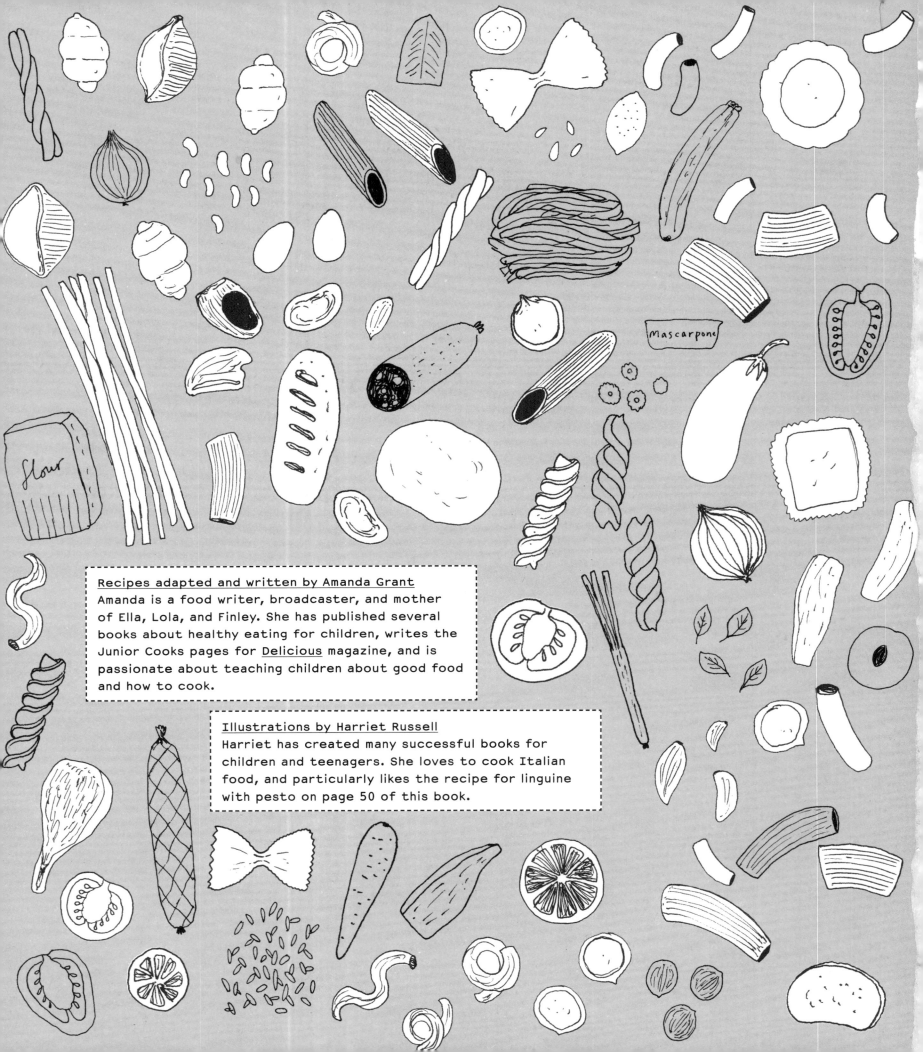

Recipes adapted and written by Amanda Grant
Amanda is a food writer, broadcaster, and mother
of Ella, Lola, and Finley. She has published several
books about healthy eating for children, writes the
Junior Cooks pages for Delicious magazine, and is
passionate about teaching children about good food
and how to cook.

Illustrations by Harriet Russell
Harriet has created many successful books for
children and teenagers. She loves to cook Italian
food, and particularly likes the recipe for linguine
with pesto on page 50 of this book.

The Silver Spoon for Children

Favourite Italian Recipes

Contents

Lunches and Snacks

pasta and Pizza

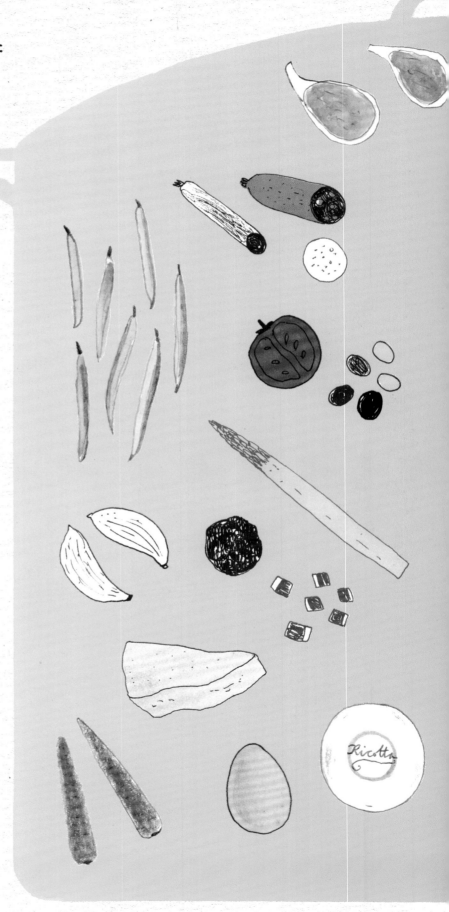

Main Courses

Desserts and Baking

Cooking the Italian way

Most people love eating Italian food, so it's fantastic if you know how to cook it! We have chosen forty recipes from The Silver Spoon, the best-selling cookbook that can be found in almost every Italian family's kitchen. We've adapted the recipes so they are very easy for you to follow. These are traditional Italian recipes that have been handed down from generation to generation, so with this book you can imagine that you are in a kitchen in Italy, learning how to cook the Italian way.

Over the centuries, Italians have discovered exactly how to mix a few simple, good quality ingredients to make meals that are full of flavour. For instance, you can make a delicious sauce for pasta with just a few basic items such as good quality tinned tomatoes, fresh basil, garlic and a good olive oil. The recipes in this book will help you learn some key skills and techniques used in any kitchen, not just Italian ones: you will learn how to use a small sharp knife (which is essential if you are going to do some proper cooking!), how to prepare vegetables, how to cook pasta, even how to make your own pizza dough from scratch.

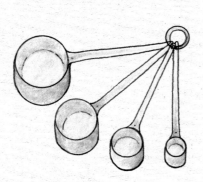

Cooking isn't just about making something good to eat: by following the recipes, you will practise some maths (measuring, sharing), reading (the recipes as well as lots of fun bits of information along the way), geography (you will learn some interesting facts about Italy) and perhaps even art (you could try drawing the food you have cooked, just like Harriet has done for the recipes in this book).

All the recipes in The Silver Spoon for Children have been tested by children – if you are aged nine or ten or older, you should be able to follow most of the recipes by yourself, with some occasional help from an adult. But do always remember to check with an adult before you begin and make sure that there is someone with you when you use a sharp knife, the oven or electrical equipment like a food processor. If you are younger than nine you will need help from an adult, or an older brother or sister. Harriet's drawings will help you along the way.

So make some time to have fun in the kitchen preparing these delicioius Italian dishes. You can then enjoy sharing your meal with family and friends – just like the Italians!

Cooking Safely

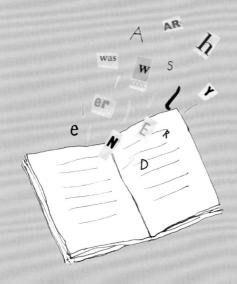

Cooking is a little like reading: once you have learnt the basics, the rest will begin to fall into place. You will learn some very useful techniques and skills in this book, but there are a few things to think about before you start, most of which I'm sure you will already know:

- Wash your hands before you start cooking, and use a hand towel or paper towel instead of drying them on your clothes. You will also need to wash your hands after handling any raw meat or fish.

- Take off any jewellery you're wearing on your hands. You don't want to bite into a piece of cake and find yourself munching on a ring!

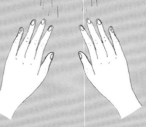

- If you have long hair, it's a good idea to tie it back. No one likes eating food with hair in it.

- Put on an apron to protect the food you're preparing from any dirt on your clothes (and to keep your clothes clean, too!).

- Always wear oven gloves when you're putting anything into the oven or taking anything out of the oven. You will also need to wear oven gloves when you're putting food under a hot grill or turning over food halfway through cooking.

- Always ask an adult to help when you use the oven or a food processor, or when you're draining pasta in a colander.

- And the most important thing: <u>Always ask an adult before you start cooking!</u>

Ring
cake

Spot the
hair in the spaghetti

Equipment and Utensils

You don't need much equipment to make the recipes in this book, but it helps to have the following:

Small sharp knife
One of the first skills all budding chefs should learn is how to use a knife properly. It's also good to learn to choose the right knife for each job. A paring knife is a good place to start – this is a small sharp knife suitable for trimming and chopping fruits and vegetables.

Did you know that a blunt knife is more dangerous than a sharp one? You have to apply a lot of pressure to cut through something with a blunt knife, but a good sharp knife glides through food easily, with less risk of it slipping. The two main cutting techniques are the bridge and the claw techniques (see page 8). Once you have mastered these, you will be able to cut most things safely, but always ask an adult before you use a sharp knife.

Chopping boards
These can be plastic or wood. Keep them clean by scrubbing them with hot water and washing-up liquid. Always wash them particularly carefully after you've put raw meat, fish or egg on them.

Wooden spoon
If you haven't got one of these I suggest you save up some pocket money and buy one – every chef needs a wooden spoon for mixing!

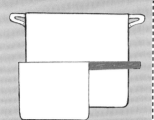

Saucepans
A couple of pans are all you need, ideally a big one for cooking pasta and a small one for making sauces. If you have a medium sized one as well, even better!

Scissors
When you use scissors to cut food like fresh herbs, always keep your fingers well away from the edges of the blades so that you don't accidentally cut yourself.

Garlic crusher
Garlic is small and can be tricky to chop. A crusher is easy to use: put a peeled garlic clove inside the cup of the crusher, then use both hands to close the crusher and push hard to squeeze the garlic out. Use a table knife to scrape the garlic off the crusher.

Food blender or processor
For some recipes, it does help if you have a food blender or processor, but if you don't have one perhaps you could borrow one from a friend. Always ask an adult to help you use a food blender, as it has a very sharp blade in the bottom. Make sure to stay away from the sharp blade, just like you would when using a sharp knife.

Pestle & mortar
A pestle and mortar are fun to use: you pound food in the mortar (the bowl) with the pestle (the heavy stick). If you don't have one, you can use the end of a wooden rolling pin to bash food in a small plastic or wooden bowl instead.

Techniques

Bridge cutting technique

Hold the piece of food you want to cut by forming a bridge with your thumb on one side and your index finger on the other. Hold the knife in your other hand with the blade facing down, guide the knife under the bridge and cut through the food. For some soft items such as tomatoes it may be easier to puncture the tomato skin with the point of the knife first before cutting.

Claw cutting technique

Place the item on the chopping board with its flat side facing down (often you will need to cut it in half first using the bridge technique). Shape the fingers of your left hand into a claw shape, tucking your thumb inside your fingers and tucking your fingertips in away from the blade. If you're left-handed, you need to make the claw with your right hand! Rest the claw on the item to be sliced. Holding the knife in your other hand, slice the item, moving the 'clawed' fingers away as the knife gets closer.

How to chop an onion

Put the onion on a chopping board. Carefully holding it in the claw cutting position, cut the pointed end off the onion. Put the onion on the board with the flat end (the end that you have just cut) sitting on the board. Hold the onion using the bridge cutting position. Cut the onion in half. Peel away the dry papery skin. To chop the onion into small pieces, known as dice, make a bridge using your fingers and thumb and then use the knife to make lots of vertical cuts through the onion from just above the root end to the top. Then switch to the claw technique and cut across the onion the other way to make small dice.

How to cut an onion into thin slices

Sit one half, flat-side down, on the chopping board. Hold the onion using the claw technique and cut across the onion to make slices.

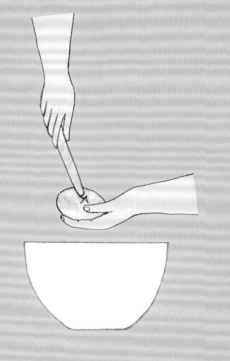

How to crack eggs
Hold the egg in one hand, almost cupping it. Hold the egg over a small bowl and hit the middle of the egg with a table knife to crack it. Put the knife down and then put your thumbs into the slit you have just made in the shell. Carefully pull the shell apart and let the egg white and yolk drop into the bowl.

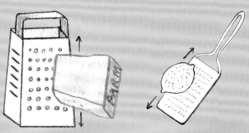

How to use a grater
Place the grater on a chopping board and hold it firmly by its handle. Hold the piece of food at its widest end and grate the food by rubbing it up and down the grater. Watch your fingers and knuckles to make sure that they don't get caught on the 'teeth' of the grater.

Have you ever noticed that a grater has different size holes in it? Sometimes you want the food to be grated into big pieces with the big holes, like grated carrots for a salad. Some foods, like Parmesan cheese, are best grated with the small holes – perfect for sprinkling over pasta!

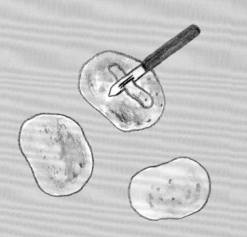

How to use a vegetable peeler
There are different types of vegetable peelers, so you might need to try a few to see which one you find easiest to handle. Hold one end of the vegetable and rest the other end on a chopping board. Starting halfway down the vegetable, run the peeler down the vegetable away from you. Be careful, as the peeler is sharp! You will need to twist the vegetable as you peel so that you peel all the way around it. Then turn the vegetable up the other way and hold the other end while you peel the other half.

How to squeeze juice from lemons and oranges
Cut the lemon or orange in half using the bridge technique (opposite). If you're feeling strong, pick up half a fruit and squeeze it over a small bowl or jug to catch the juice. Or if you have a squeezer like the one in this illustration, you can put the orange or lemon half on it and push down, twisting the fruit at the same time, to squeeze the juice out of the fruit.

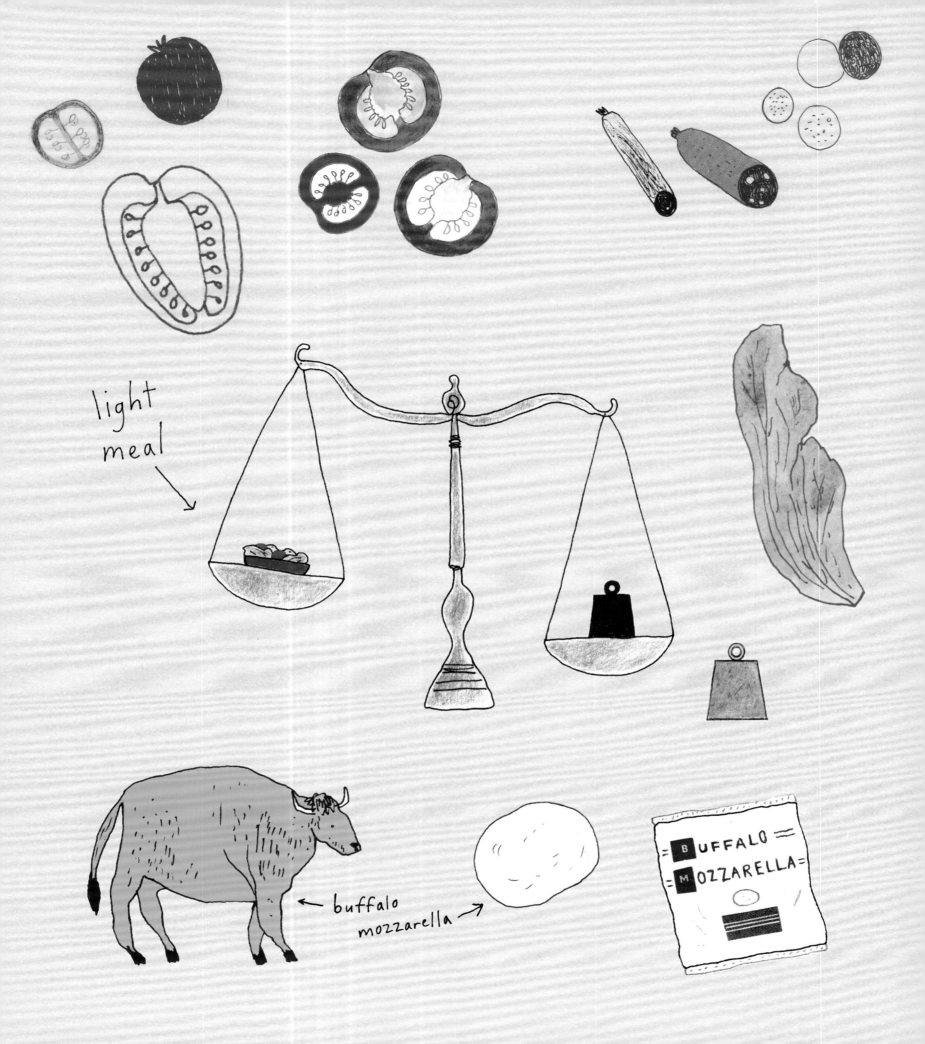

light meal

buffalo mozzarella

=BUFFALO=
=MOZZARELLA=

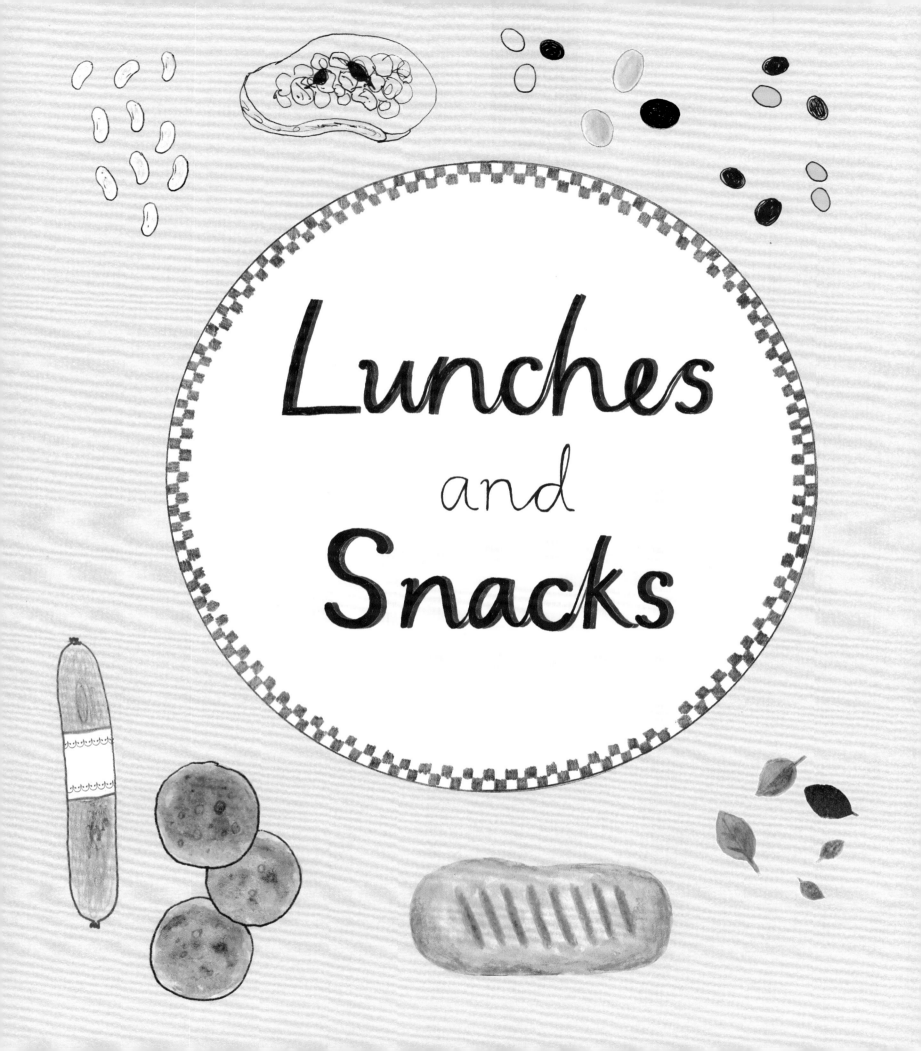

Lunches
and
Snacks

Prosciutto and Melon

Prosciutto (pronounced 'pro-shoo-toe') is a delicious kind of ham, and its salty flavour goes really well with the sweet melon in this popular starter or antipasto. Choose small ripe melons for this recipe so that they are easy to cut. Cantaloupe and Honeydew are best, but any type is good. Cantaloupes are round, with pale green bumpy skin and delicious orange flesh inside. Honeydew melons are often bigger and slightly more oval, and have yellowy green skin and pale green flesh.

<u>Makes enough for 4 people as a starter</u>
Or serve with crusty bread as a light lunch

– 2 small, ripe melons*
– 8–12 slices of prosciutto
  (2 or 3 slices for each person)

* To check if the melons are ripe, smell them – they should smell of melon!

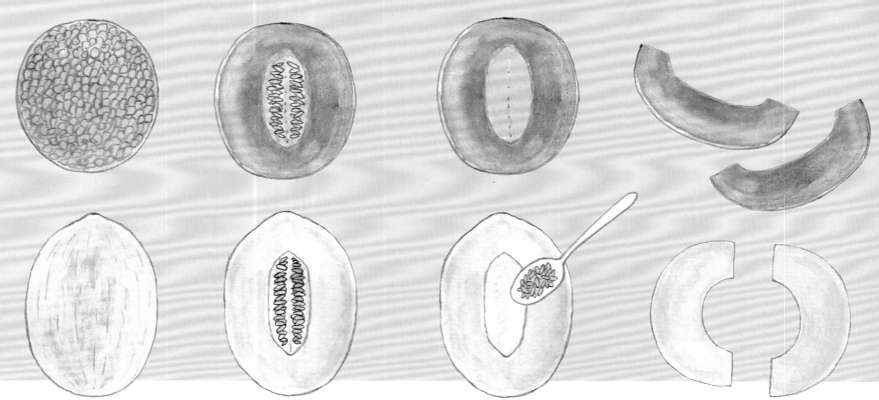

❶ Cut the melons in half using the bridge technique (see page 8). You will need to almost saw through the fruit to cut it, so be careful as you go – always keep your fingers in the bridge position, so that the knife is well away from your fingers. You may need an adult to help you cut the melons.

❷ Using a dessertspoon, scoop the seeds out of the melon and throw them away.

❸ Using the bridge technique, cut the melon into quarters by cutting each melon half in half again.

salty

+

sweet

4 You can just serve the melon on its skin and eat it with a knife and fork, or you can use a spoon to scoop out the flesh. Alternatively, you can make the melon easier to eat by using the bridge technique to cut a crisscross pattern in its flesh, but without cutting all the way through the skin.

5 You will need four plates. Put two pieces of melon onto each plate, followed by two or three slices of prosciutto.

6 You can try draping the prosciutto over the melon pieces – you always want to make sure that the food looks good, so that your friends or family enjoy eating it. Serve with a knife and fork or a spoon.

TOMATO Bruschetta

<u>Makes enough for 4 people as a starter</u>
You might need to make more if you want to eat this for lunch

- 1 small rustic loaf
  or 1 small baguette
- 4 tablespoons extra-virgin
  olive oil for drizzling
- 8 ripe plum tomatoes
- 1 clove garlic
- freshly ground black pepper
  (optional)
- a few fresh basil leaves
  (optional)

Bruschetta (pronounced 'broos-ketta') was originally invented as a good way of using up stale bread by toasting it and adding a range of delicious toppings. The simplest one is made with juicy, ripe tomatoes, and many Italians would say it's the best! You could also try toppings such as mozzarella cheese, basil, ham or roasted vegetables.

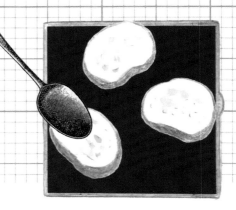

❶ Turn the oven on to 180°C／350°F／Gas Mark 4. Using a serrated knife (a knife with a jagged edge) use the claw cutting technique (see page 8) to slice the bread

into 8 slices. Try to cut the bread slightly diagonally so that the slices have an oval shape. You might want to ask an adult to cut it for you.

❷ Lay the bread flat on a baking tray. Using a spoon, drizzle 2 tablespoons of oil over all the slices – it won't cover the bread, just drip over it in places.

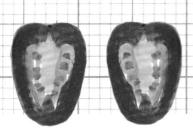

❺ For the tomato topping, cut a ripe plum tomato in half length-ways using the bridge technique (see page 8). Put a tomato half on a chopping board, with its flat side facing down.

❻ Again using the bridge technique, cut the tomato half into long thin strips, then move your fingers into the claw position and cut the long strips into little pieces.

This is called dicing. The diced tomatoes should be in tiny squares, but it doesn't matter if they are different sizes – they will still taste great!

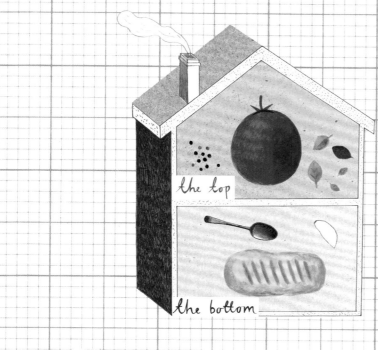

the top

the bottom

10 mins

❸ Wearing your oven gloves, put the tray into the oven. After 10 minutes, take the tray out, carefully turn the bread over and then put back into the oven for another 10 minutes.

❹ The bread should now be a light golden colour and crisp. Take the bread out of the oven and rest the tray on a pan stand. Leave to cool slightly.

Rub

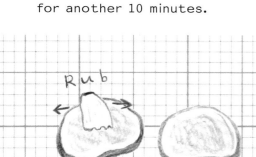

❼ Peel the papery skin away from the garlic clove. Pick up a slice of toasted bread and rub both sides with the garlic. Do the same with the other slices of toasted bread.

❽ Put the toasted bread on a big plate, divide the tomatoes among them and drizzle with the remaining olive oil. If you like, you could sprinkle some black pepper over the top, too, or some fresh basil leaves, torn into small pieces.

Sausage Crostini

Crostini are little toasts with different toppings. This one, with sausage meat and Taleggio cheese, makes a great lunch dish with green salad leaves. Taleggio is a soft cheese from northern Italy, where people used to leave it in caves in the mountains to ripen. You can have fun crushing the fennel seeds for this recipe, either with a pestle and mortar (see page 7) or with a rolling pin.

Makes enough for 4 people
- 3 good quality pork sausages
- 1 teaspoon fennel seeds
- 125 g Taleggio cheese, or any other cheese you like that will melt easily
- 8 slices rustic bread

❶ Turn the oven on to 180°C/350°F/ Gas Mark 4. Using scissors (see page 7), snip the sausages to open the skin and squeeze the sausage meat into a bowl.

❷ Put the fennel seeds into a mortar and grind with a pestle to crush the seeds, or put the seeds into a small plastic or wooden bowl and crush them with the end of a rolling pin. Stir the crushed fennel seeds into the sausage meat.

❸ Carefully peel the rind away from the cheese and throw the rind away. Break the cheese into small chunks.

CRUSH

grind

Taleggio caves

Is it ready yet?

MIX

4 Put the cheese into the bowl with the sausage meat and use a spoon or a fork to mix everything together.

5 Cut the slices of bread in half using the bridge technique (see page 8). Put the bread onto a baking tray (you might need two trays) and spread a layer of sausage mixture onto each slice, like a thick layer of jam.

6 Wearing your oven gloves, put the baking tray (or trays) in the oven, and cook for 15 minutes. The bread should be slightly crisp and toasted, the sausages will be cooked and the cheese will have melted.

Pizzaiola toasts

This is a great starter or light lunch on a summer's day. You can get everything ready beforehand and then spoon the mixture onto the toasts when you are ready to eat. These are quite messy to eat, so you could put the filling between two pieces of toast to make a sandwich.

Makes enough for 4 people
- 2 firm ripe tomatoes
- 2 spring onions
- 6 green olives
- 2 sprigs fresh flat-leaf parsley
- a few fresh oregano leaves
- 1 tablespoon extra-virgin olive oil
- about 8 slices white bread (or fewer if the slices are very big)
- 125 g mozzarella cheese

❶ Cut the tomatoes in half using the bridge technique (see page 8) and scoop out the seeds with a teaspoon. Using the claw technique (see page 8), cut the tomato flesh into thin strips and then cut each strip into small square pieces, like little dice. Put the small tomato pieces into a bowl.

❷ Using the claw technique, trim the spring onions by cutting off the roots and the dark green part of the other ends. Then cut the spring onions into thin slices and add to the tomatoes.

❸ Using a rolling pin, carefully squash an olive slightly, so you can open it up and take the stone out. Do this with all the olives.

❹ Using the bridge technique, cut the olives into quarters and add to the tomatoes. Pull the herb leaves off the stalks, then using scissors (see page 7) snip the parsley and oregano into small pieces. Add half of the herbs and oil to the tomatoes and mix with a spoon.

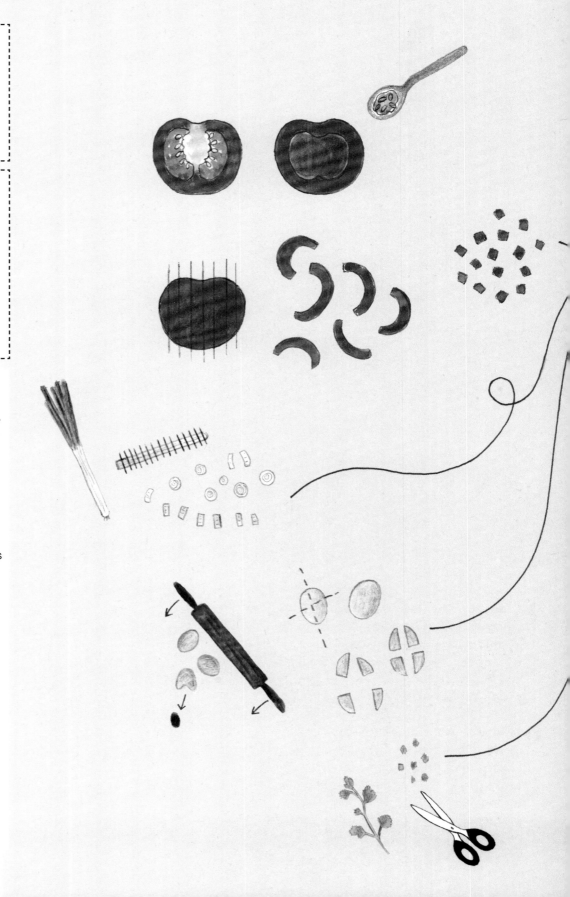

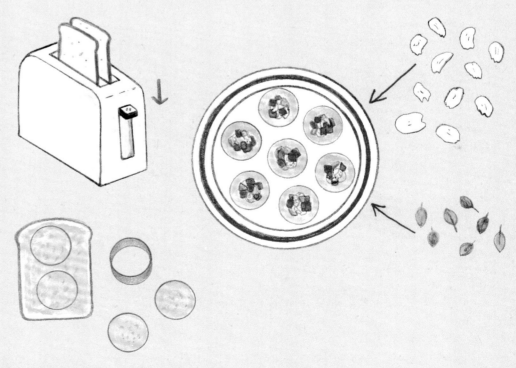

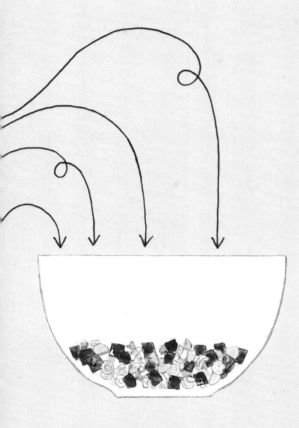

5 Toast the bread in a toaster. Using a biscuit cutter (about 6 cm in diameter), cut circles out of the toast – how many circles you can make will depend on how big your slices of toast are.

6 Take the mozzarella cheese out its liquid and tear the cheese into small pieces. Put the circles of toast onto a big plate. Divide the tomato mixture among the toasts and top with mozzarella. Scatter the fresh herbs over the toasts and enjoy!

Panzanella Salad

Makes enough for 4 people
- 6 slices home-made or rustic bread
- 2 tablespoons red wine vinegar
- 4 really ripe and juicy tomatoes
- freshly ground black pepper
- 6 basil leaves
- 3 tablespoons extra-virgin olive oil
- olives, chopped cucumber, red onions or spring onions (optional). You could try adding a handful of each or any of these to the salad

Like bruschetta (see page 14), panzanella was invented as a way to use up old bread. Nowadays, Italian cooks often like to add olives or chopped cucumber, red onion or spring onion to this traditional salad, so you might like to try adding these, too.

Panzanella is even tastier if you prepare it a few hours before you want to eat it, so that the bread can absorb the flavour of the tomatoes. You will need firm, tasty rustic bread with a coarse texture and really ripe tomatoes with lots of flavour.

ugghh...

Yum!

Old stale loaf ..... becomes....... Delicious refreshing salad!

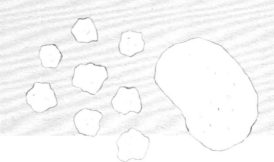

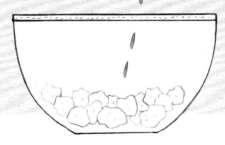

❶ Cut or tear the crusts off slices of bread.

❷ Break the bread into small pieces and put into a bowl.

❸ Sprinkle a little red wine vinegar over the bread. This adds a bit of flavour and makes the bread nice and moist.

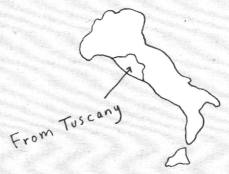

From Tuscany

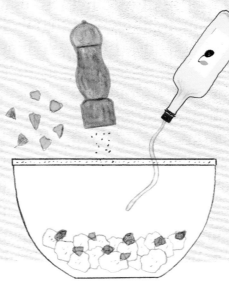

4 Roughly chop the tomatoes into small pieces using the bridge and claw cutting techniques (see page 8).

5 Add a pinch of freshly ground black pepper to the bread. Tear the basil leaves and sprinkle them over the bread, then drizzle over the olive oil.

6 Add the tomatoes and any other ingredients you might like to add. Using two forks or a big spoon, mix everything together. If you can, wait a few hours for the flavours to mingle before eating – it will taste even better.

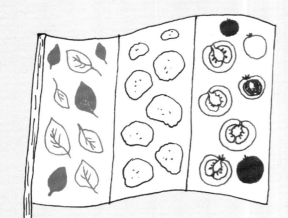

Italian flag

Mozzarella

This simple salad is delicious served with crusty bread to mop up the juices. The recipe originally comes from the island of Capri in southern Italy. That's the same region that pizza comes from, and tomatoes, mozzarella and basil are also important ingredients in many traditional pizza toppings.

It's best to use really ripe tomatoes for this recipe, so choose them carefully – they should be deep red and smell like tomatoes! It doesn't matter if your tomato slices aren't all the same shape or thickness, they will still taste delicious. Keep tomatoes in the kitchen, not the fridge, so that they continue to ripen and taste good.

Makes enough for 4 people
- 4 ripe tomatoes
- 250 g mozzarella cheese
- 8 fresh basil leaves
- 2 tablespoons extra-virgin olive oil

❶ Cut the ripe tomatoes into rings using the bridge technique (see page 8). Try to cut them as thin as you can, but it really doesn't matter if they are not all the same thickness. You may find it easier to first cut the tomatoes in half widthways, also using the bridge technique. Then place the tomato halves cut side down on a chopping board and slice them into thin strips using the claw cutting technique. This way, you end up with half circles rather than rings.

❷ Take the mozzarella cheese out of its liquid (this liquid helps to keep the cheese fresh). Carefully tear the cheese into pretty pieces. If your mozzarella is very soft, you can almost peel the cheese to make delicate petal shapes.

❸ Scatter the tomatoes and cheese on the plate in any way you choose – your plate should have a lovely mixture of red and white on it. Tear the basil leaves and sprinkle them over the top, then drizzle over the olive oil. Keep cool until you are ready to eat.

and tomato Salad

Summer Cannellini bean Salad

Cannellini beans are especially popular in a region of Italy called Tuscany. People who live there are sometimes even called <u>mangia-fagioli</u>, or 'bean-eaters'! This cannellini bean salad is perfect for a light summer lunch, or as a side dish with cooked chicken or sausages. It would be tasty in a packed lunch, too. This is a great recipe for practising chopping with a small knife, as you start by dicing the vegetables – this means cutting them into small pieces.

<u>Makes enough for 4 people</u>
- 1 aubergine
- 1 yellow pepper
- 2 ripe tomatoes
- 1 clove garlic
- 2 tablespoons extra-virgin olive oil
- 400 g tin cannellini beans, drained and rinsed
- 1 lemon
- 4 fresh basil leaves
- 1 sprig fresh flat-leaf parsley

❶ Dice the aubergine: using the bridge technique (see page 8), cut the aubergine in half widthways and then cut each half in half again lengthways. Rest the quarters flat side down on a chopping board and, using the bridge technique, cut each quarter into thin strips. Using the claw technique (see page 8) cut each aubergine strip into small pieces.

❷ Dice the pepper using the same techniques as for the aubergine: cut the pepper in half and remove the seeds and white part, then cut it into strips. Cut the strips of pepper into small pieces.

 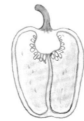   

❸ Then dice the tomatoes in the same way: cut the tomatoes in half, rest them cut side down on a board and cut into thin strips. Cut each strip into small pieces.

Bean eaters

4 Peel the papery skin away from the garlic clove. Put the oil in a heavy-based saucepan, add the garlic clove, aubergine and pepper and cook over a low heat for about 10 minutes until the pepper is slightly soft, stirring occasionally.

5 Add the tomatoes and beans, cover and cook very gently for 15 minutes, stirring every now and then.

6 Take the pan off the heat and use a fork to take out the garlic and throw it away.

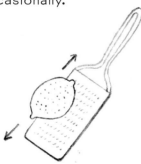

7 Carefully grate the yellow peel of the lemon to make lemon zest, keeping your fingers well away from the grater (see page 9). Don't grate the white pith under the yellow skin – it tastes bitter!

8 Tear the basil leaves into small pieces and snip the parsley leaves into small pieces using scissors (see page 7).

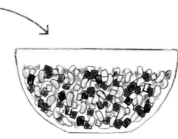

9 Spoon the beans and vegetables into a big serving bowl. Scatter the lemon zest and herbs over the beans, mix everything together and eat. This dish tastes good warm or cold.

Tuna and bean Salad

Makes enough for 4 people
- 1 small thin leek or 1 spring onion
- 1 ripe tomato
- 1 small lettuce or 1 head escarole
- 4 small tuna steaks (or 2 × 185 g tins of tuna in oil, drained)
- 2 tablespoons olive oil
- 1 clove garlic
- 10 fresh basil leaves
- 40 g pine nuts
- 400 g tin cannellini beans, drained and rinsed

You can use tinned tuna instead of fresh for this salad, and you can add any fresh ingredients you have in your fridge or growing in your garden. This salad tastes so good because you rub garlic around the salad bowl and add crunchy pine nuts and fresh basil leaves. You might like to drizzle a little lemon juice over the top, too. That's the great thing about making salads: you can change the ingredients and make your very own creation!

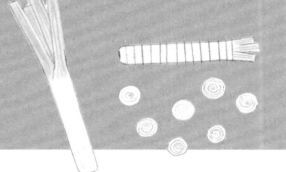

1 Trim the ends off the leek or spring onion and then slice it thinly using the claw cutting technique (see page 8).

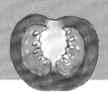

2 Using the bridge technique (see page 8), cut the tomato in half and scoop out the seeds using a teaspoon.

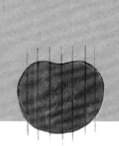

3 Using the claw technique, thinly slice the tomato halves.

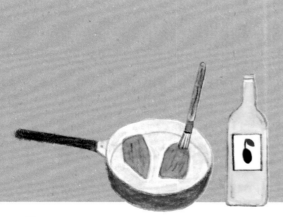

5 You will need an adult to help you cook the tuna steaks (If you're using tinned tuna, go to step 6). Heat a griddle pan or frying pan, brush the tuna with a little oil and put into the pan.

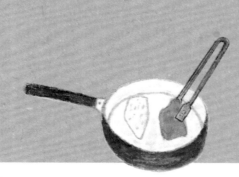

6 Cook for 2 minutes, use tongs to turn over and cook for another 2 minutes – the tuna will still be slightly pink in the middle. You can cook it for longer if you prefer it not to be too pink.

7 Cut the garlic in half and rub it around the sides of a salad bowl. Tear the basil leaves and put into the bowl together with the pine nuts. Drizzle the oil over the nuts and herbs and mix well with a spoon.

4 Tear or finely slice the lettuce or escarole using the claw cutting technique.

That looks good....

8 Add the beans, leek or spring onion, tomato and lettuce or escarole and gently mix everything together.

9 If you're using tinned tuna, break it into chunks and mix them into the beans. If you're using fresh tuna, you can serve the cooked tuna steaks alongside the salad, or slice them into chunks using the bridge technique and mix them in.

Tuscan Minestrone Soup

Makes enough for 4 people

- 2 leeks
- 1 carrot
- 1 celery stick
- 1 courgette
- 2 sprigs fresh flat-leaf parsley
- 2 tablespoons olive oil, plus a little extra to drizzle over the finished soup
- 400 g tin chopped tomatoes
- 1 sprig fresh rosemary
- 400 g tin cannellini beans, drained and rinsed
- 1 litre vegetable stock or water (if you are not using fresh stock, use a good vegetable stock powder)
- 80 g long-grain rice
- 25 g Parmesan cheese

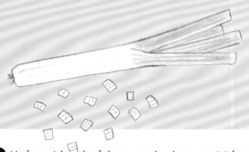  

❶ Using the bridge and claw cutting techniques (see page 8), trim the roots from the bottom and the dark green leaves from the top of the leeks. Then cut the leeks, carrot, celery and courgette in half widthways, then in half lengthways. Cut each half into thin strips lengthways. Using the claw technique (see page 8), cut the thin strips of carrot, celery, courgette and leek into small pieces.

❸ Put the oil, carrot, celery and parsley in a saucepan and cook over a very low gentle heat for about 10 minutes, stirring every now and then with a wooden spoon.

❹ Add the courgette, leek and chopped tomatoes to the mixture and cook for another 10 minutes, stirring every now and then.

❺ Pick the leaves off the sprig of fresh rosemary. Add the beans, rosemary and stock and bring to the boil.

Minestrone is a popular vegetable soup, which often has beans, rice or pasta in it, too. It can be made with just about any of your favourite vegetables, as long as they are chopped up small: it's the small pieces that make the soup a proper minestrone. Sprinkled with grated Parmesan cheese and drizzled with olive oil, it makes a really tasty lunch or supper. Make sure you grate the Parmesan carefully, keeping your fingers well away from the grater!

2 Using scissors (see page 7), snip the parsley into small pieces.

6 Add the rice and cook for another 15–20 minutes until the rice is cooked. To check if it's ready, taste a little rice with a teaspoon – remember it will be hot! It should be tender, but still have a little 'bite' in the middle.

7 You will need an adult to help you very carefully ladle half of the soup into a food processor and blend until smooth. Pour back into the pan and stir.

8 Carefully grate the Parmesan (see page 9) and sprinkle over the top. Drizzle over some olive oil.

Tuna frittata and green beans with tomato

Makes enough for 4 people

For the fritatta:
- 1 spring onion
- 6 free-range eggs
- 1 sprig fresh flat-leaf parsley
- 25 g butter
- 185 g tin of tuna in oil, drained

For the green beans with tomato:
- 1 spring onion
- 600 g green beans
- 6 green olives
- 1 tablespoon extra-virgin olive oil
- 1 clove garlic

- 400 g tin chopped tomatoes
- 6 fresh basil leaves
- freshly ground black pepper

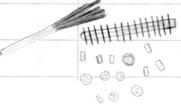

1 Using the bridge and claw cutting techniques (see page 8), trim the roots from the bottom and dark green leaves from the top of the spring onion and then finely slice the spring onion.

2 Crack the eggs into a bowl (see page 9) and whisk lightly with a fork. Using scissors, snip the parsley into small pieces and add to the eggs. Turn the grill on to high.

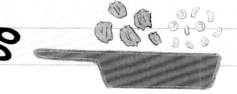

3 Melt the butter in a frying pan and fry the spring onion gently over a medium heat for 5 minutes until soft. Add the tuna and stir gently.

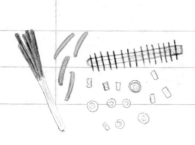

1 For the green beans with tomato: using the bridge and claw cutting techniques (see page 8), trim the roots from the bottom and dark green leaves from the top of the spring onion and then finely slice the spring onion. Trim the ends off the beans.

2 Using a rolling pin, carefully squash an olive slightly, so you can open it up and take the stone out. Do this with all the olives.

3 Half-fill a pan with water. Put the green beans into a steamer or colander and put it on top of the pan, over the water. Cover with a lid. Bring to the boil and steam the beans for 3-4 minutes. Take off the heat.

Frittata is a type of omelette. It's delicious served hot or cold, making it a great lunch or picnic dish. The first time you make a frittata, you might prefer to just serve it with a salad, but when you are more confident about cooking one, you can try making the beans and tomatoes to go with it, too. You could also try adding other ingredients such as chopped ham or crumbled cheese instead of tuna. If you decide to make both parts of this recipe, make the beans with tomato first and leave them to one side while you cook the frittata.

4 Turn the heat up slightly and pour the egg mixture over the tuna and onion. Move the egg around in the pan a few times to help it cook, then leave for 2–3 minutes until the bottom of the frittata is cooked.

5 Wearing your oven gloves, put the pan under the grill for 2–3 minutes until the egg is cooked all the way through and is golden and bubbly on top. Serve with the green beans with tomato.

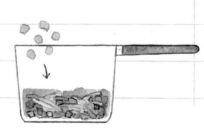

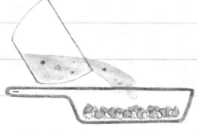

4 Put the oil, spring onion and garlic in a saucepan and cook over a low heat for 5 minutes, stirring occasionally.

5 Using a fork, fish out the whole garlic clove. Add the beans, chopped tomatoes and olives, and season with a little freshly ground black pepper.

6 Tear the basil into pieces and add, then simmer over a low heat for 2–3 minutes.

31

Tagliatelle nest

pizza cutter unicycle

A pizza fit for a Queen

pasta

and

Pizza

ITALY

Pizza Dough

Pizza has been popular in Italy for hundreds of years, and is now popular around the world. Once you have mastered making pizza dough, you can have fun with lots of different toppings – look at pages 36–37 for ideas.

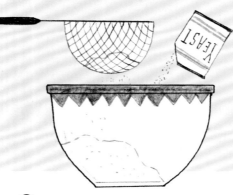

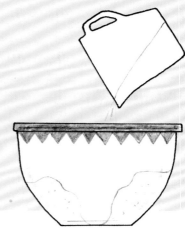

1 You will need 150 ml warm water, so first measure 75 ml cold water in a measuring jug and then add 75 ml hot water. Dip your finger in to test the temperature – it should just feel warm.

2 Sift the flour into a really big bowl. Sprinkle the dried yeast over it.

3 Make a well – a big hole – in the middle of the flour, deep enough so that you can see the bottom of the bowl. Pour the warm water and olive oil into the well.

GROWS

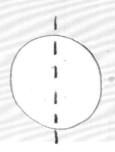

6 Wash and dry your bowl. Shape your dough into a big ball, put into the bowl and cover with a clean tea towel. Leave in a warm place for about 1 hour, until it has doubled in size – watch it grow!

7 Using a pastry brush, brush 2 large baking trays with a little oil or cut 2 pieces of baking paper to fit the trays.

8 Sprinkle a little flour over the work surface. Take the dough out of the bowl and cut it in half with a table knife.

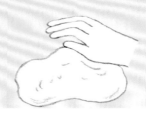

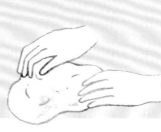

❹ Use a wooden spoon to mix everything to a soft dough.

❺ Sprinkle a little flour over your work surface and place the dough onto the flour. Knead the dough by pushing it away from you with the base of your hands and then pulling it back with your fingers. Keep doing this for about 5 minutes until you can stretch the dough like a big piece of elastic.

❾ Flatten each half with your hands and a rolling pin, and shape it into a big circle about the size of a large dinner plate, about 5 mm thick. Do the same with the other half of the dough to make 2 circles.

❿ Lift the dough onto your baking trays — you may need to ask someone to help you with this! You are now ready to add your toppings.

Note: Italians like to sift the flour straight onto a work surface instead of using a bowl. It can get a bit messy, but when you have made this dough successfully a few times in a bowl, you might like to try this, too!

In 1889, when Italy still had a king and queen, Queen Margherita asked a chef to cook her a pizza. He used ingredients that matched the Italian flag: red tomatoes, white mozzarella and green basil.

If you like, you can scatter some Parmesan cheese over your Pizza Margherita for extra flavour when it comes out of the oven. It's not strictly authentic, but it tastes good! Pizza Napoletana, which was invented in Naples, is another very traditional topping. Sausage pizza is not as traditional as those two toppings, but the sausages and pancetta (pronounced 'pan-chetta'), a type of cured bacon, are very tasty with the rosemary.

If you don't have fresh ripe tomatoes, these pizzas will still taste great just using passata, which is a sieved tomato puree with a lovely flavour.

Pizza Margherita

Queen Margherita

Makes 2 big pizzas
- 2 pizza bases (see page 34)
- 4–5 tablespoons tomato passata
- 4 ripe tomatoes
- 150 g mozzarella cheese
- 6 fresh basil leaves, plus a few extra
- handful of freshly grated Parmesan cheese (optional)

❶ Turn the oven on to 200°C/400°F/Gas Mark 7. Spread 2–3 tablespoons passata over each base using the back of a spoon. Using the bridge technique (see page 8) cut the tomatoes in half, and then cut the flesh into slices using the claw technique (see page 8). Divide the tomato slices between the two bases.

❷ Tear the mozzarella into pieces and scatter the pieces of cheese over the tomatoes. Tear the basil leaves and scatter over the top. You are now ready to bake your pizzas! Using your oven gloves put both pizza trays in the oven. Bake for 15–20 minutes, until the bases are golden and cooked. Tear a few more basil leaves and scatter over the top before you serve.

Pizza Napoletana

Makes 2 big pizzas
- 2 pizza bases (see page 34)
- 4–5 tablespoons tomato passata
- 4 ripe tomatoes
- 150 g mozzarella cheese
- 8 tinned anchovy fillets, drained
- pinch of dried oregano

1 Turn the oven on to 200°C/400°F/ Gas Mark 7. Follow step 1 as for Pizza Margherita. Then tear the mozzarella into pieces and scatter the cheese over the tomatoes.

2 With their strong salty taste, anchovies are an important ingredient in this pizza, but if you're trying them for the first time, use half the amount suggested here. First tear the anchovies into small pieces and scatter them over the top, then the oregano. To bake, see step 2 for Pizza Margherita.

Sausage Pizza

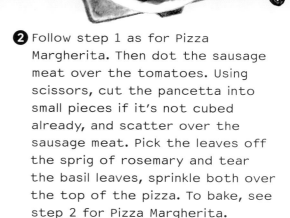

Makes 2 big pizzas
- 2 pizza bases (see page 34)
- 200 g good quality sausages
- 50 g pecorino cheese
- freshly ground black pepper
- 4–5 tablespoons tomato passata
- 4 ripe tomatoes
- 100 g pancetta slices or cubes
- 1 sprig fresh rosemary
- a few fresh basil leaves

1 Turn the oven on to 200°C/400°F/ Gas Mark 7. Using scissors (see page 7), snip open the sausage skin and squeeze the sausage meat into a bowl. Grate the pecorino carefully, making sure that your fingers stay well away from the grater (see page 9). Add the grated cheese, season with a little freshly ground black pepper and mix with a spoon.

2 Follow step 1 as for Pizza Margherita. Then dot the sausage meat over the tomatoes. Using scissors, cut the pancetta into small pieces if it's not cubed already, and scatter over the sausage meat. Pick the leaves off the sprig of rosemary and tear the basil leaves, sprinkle both over the top of the pizza. To bake, see step 2 for Pizza Margherita.

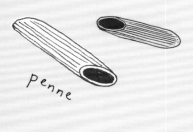

Penne

pasta

macaroni

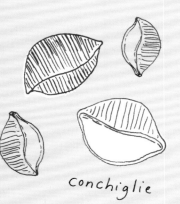

Conchiglie

Pasta is a staple food in Italy. Many people have special big, deep saucepans with lids they only use for cooking pasta. You need a big pan because pasta swells and expands as it cooks, and needs plenty of room to move around. If there is not enough room in the pan, the pasta at the bottom will cook quicker than the rest. Some modern pasta pans even have a large colander inside them, ready to drain the pasta when it is cooked.

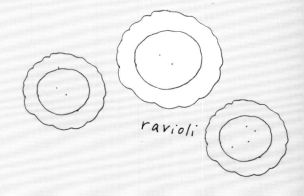

ravioli

Cappelletti

Pasta comes in all kinds of different shapes and sizes with great names: short pastas include <u>cappelletti</u>, which means 'little hats', and <u>farfalle</u>, which means 'butterflies'. Long pastas include <u>linguine</u>, which means 'little tongues', and <u>capellini</u>, which means 'fine hair' – this is the thinnest, wispiest pasta you will ever see.
How many different types of pasta can you think of? How many have you tasted?

farfalle

linguine

Pasta is quick and easy to cook, so it's perfect if you are in a hurry. There are two main types of pasta, fresh and dried. Fresh pasta is usually made with flour and eggs (see page 40) and only keeps for a few days, while dried pasta is usually made just with flour and water, and can be stored for months.

Cappellini

Italians take their pasta very seriously and never overcook it. They boil the pasta until it is cooked but still has a firm texture or 'bite' to it, rather than being fully soft. They call this '<u>al dente</u>', which means 'to the tooth'.

tagliatelle

lumache

Fusilli

Rigatoni

How to cook dried pasta

❶ Fill the biggest saucepan you can find three-quarters full with cold water. You will need to an adult to help you carry it to the hob. Bring the water to the boil over a high heat.

❷ Carefully add the pasta and stir well. Stir occasionally with a long handled spoon to prevent it from sticking. Cook the pasta for 1 minute less than it recommends on the pack, as it's always better that the pasta is slightly under-cooked rather than overcooked and soggy. Use a fork to take a piece of pasta from the pan, leave to cool slightly and then test to see if it is ready – it should be cooked but still have a little 'bite'.

❸ You will need an adult to help you drain the pasta in a colander. Serve the pasta immediately, with the sauce of your choice.

Fresh Pasta dough

You only need two ingredients to make your own fresh pasta – flour and eggs. Italians believe the best flour for pasta-making is a variety called 00 ('doppio zero' or double zero), which is very fine and perfect for making a smooth dough. If you can't find this type of flour, try using strong bread flour instead. To give your pasta the best flavour and colour, use eggs from hens that have been free to roam and eat grass and corn. Making fresh pasta by hand is great fun. In Italy they make it straight on a work surface or table, but it's best to start by making it in a bowl first. Once you're confident that you know what you're doing, you could try making it the Italian way. Freshly-made pasta is great with all the different sauces in this book, from tomato sauce (see page 46) to pesto (see page 50).

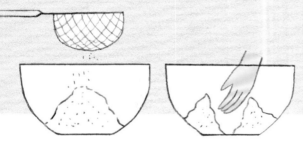

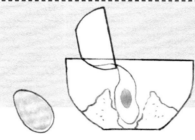

1 Sift the flour into a big bowl or onto a clean work surface if you're feeling very confident. Scoop out the middle of the flour to make a small well – you should be able to see the bottom of the bowl.

2 Crack the eggs into a bowl (see page 9). Pour the eggs into the well. Now use the fingertips of one hand as a spoon to mix the yolks and whites together. Keep stirring slowly: as you stir, the flour will gradually fall into the egg until it is all mixed in.

3 You can now use both hands to bring all the flour and egg together to make a ball of dough. If you're finding it hard to bring the flour together, wet your hands with some water and then carry on mixing the dough.

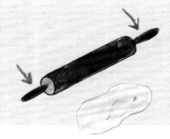

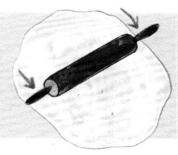

6 Now for the rolling. Cut the dough in half – it's easier to roll out 2 smaller pieces. Wrap one half back up in the damp tea towel, to keep it moist. Sprinkle some flour over your rolling pin and a clean work surface and start to roll one piece of dough. Keep rolling, turning the dough so that it doesn't stick to the table – you may need to lift it up and sprinkle more flour underneath the dough as you roll. You want to roll the pasta dough until it is really thin – about as big as an A4 piece of paper and as thin as possible. If you have a pasta machine, you can use this to roll the pasta out for you.

4 Once you have a big ball of dough, you're ready to start kneading. A great way to knead is to put the dough on a clean floured surface, push it down with the bottom of your hand, then fold the dough over and push down again. Keep turning the dough and pushing and stretching and you will end up with a smooth ball of dough. If your arms start to feel tired, ask someone else to have a go! It will take about 10–15 minutes before the dough is smooth and elastic. If you stop too soon, the dough may tear when you roll it out.

5 Give yourself and the dough a rest! Wrap the dough in a damp clean tea towel and leave it for 30 minutes to 1 hour in the kitchen.

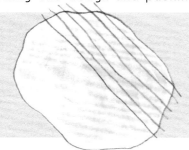 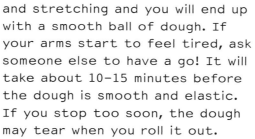 

7 Use a small sharp knife to cut the fresh pasta. To make tagliatelle, which look like ribbons, cut the dough into long strips about 5 mm wide. It doesn't matter if they aren't perfectly straight, they will still taste just as good.

8 Three-quarters fill a large pan with water and bring to the boil. Carefully add the fresh pasta and cook for only 3–4 minutes until it's just done. The pasta should be soft, and should not taste 'raw'. Ask an adult to help you drain the pasta in a colander.

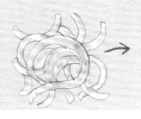 

Yellow yolk = Yellow pasta

Ravioli Napoletana

Makes enough for 4 people
- 1 quantity tomato sauce
  (see page 46)

For the fresh pasta dough:
- 300 g Italian type 00 flour
  or strong bread flour
- 3 large free-range eggs

For the filling:
- 100 g ricotta cheese
- 100 g cooked ham
- 1 sprig fresh flat-leaf parsley
- 1 free-range egg
- 100 g mozzarella cheese
- 100 g Parmesan cheese

Ravioli are little pasta shapes that look a bit like miniature pillows, and they can be filled with many different things. Once you've practised this recipe, you can try using different fillings such as cooked pumpkin and ricotta cheese.

❶ Make the tomato sauce by following steps 1 to 5 on pages 46–47 and put to one side. You will need it later to serve with the finished ravioli.

❷ Make the pasta dough by following steps 1 to 3 of the basic recipe on pages 40–41. You will need more flour and eggs, but the way you make the dough is the same. Cover the dough with a damp tea towel and leave to rest for 30 minutes.

❸ To make the filling, put the ricotta in a bowl and beat with a wooden spoon. Tear the ham into small pieces or, using scissors (see page 7), snip the ham into small pieces and add to the ricotta.

❼ Three-quarters fill a large pan with water and bring to the boil. Then keep it just gently simmering, so that you're ready to cook the pasta as soon as you have finished making it.

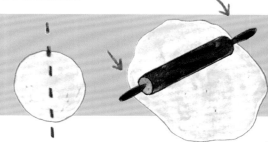

❽ Take the pasta dough you made earlier, cut it in half and wrap one half back up in the damp tea towel. Always keep pasta dough covered when you're not using it to keep it moist. Roll one half of the pasta dough to the size of an A4 sheet of paper, as thinly as you can.

❾ Using a biscuit cutter or a glass, cut circles of dough from the sheet. Start at one end and work your way across, to make as many circles as possible. You need to do this quite quickly so the pasta doesn't dry out. You will need an even number of circles – 16 would be good.

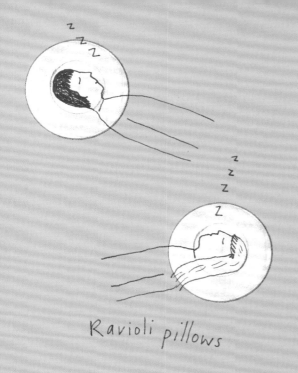

Ravioli pillows

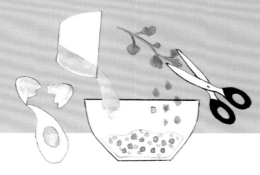

4 Using scissors, snip the parsley leaves into small pieces and add to the ricotta. Crack the egg into a small bowl (see page 7) and whisk with a fork. Tip the egg onto the cheese.

5 Take the mozzarella out of its liquid and then tear it into small pieces and add to the ricotta.

6 Grate the Parmesan carefully, keeping your fingers away from the grater (see page 9), and add to the ricotta. Mix everything together, cover and keep in the fridge until you need it.

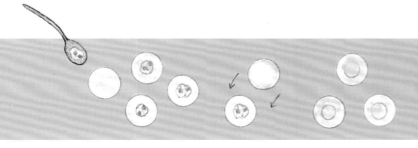

10 Fill a small bowl with water. Spoon a little filling into the middle of 8 of the circles of pasta, wet a finger with water from the bowl and use to moisten the edges of the ravioli. Top with the other 8 circles so that you have a total of 8 ravioli. Very carefully use your fingers to gently press the edges of the pasta circles together, making sure that you don't have any air pockets. This is an important stage – if the piece of ravioli isn't sealed properly, the filling may come out when you cook the ravioli. Repeat with the other half of pasta dough and the rest of the filling.

11 Cook the ravioli for about 5 minutes or until they rise to the top of the water. Use a slotted spoon to carefully take one out of the boiling water and test if it is cooked. The pasta should be soft and should not taste 'raw'. Serve the ravioli with the tomato sauce.

Tagliatelle with Cream, peas and ham

Makes enough for 4 people
- 1 quantity fresh pasta dough (see page 40) or 400g dried tagliatelle
- 1 onion or 2 spring onions
- 10g butter
- 2 teaspoons olive oil
- 200g shelled fresh peas (or frozen peas if you don't have fresh)
- 2 slices cooked ham
- 100ml double cream
- 40g Parmesan cheese

This is a delicious sauce for fresh homemade tagliatelle, but it's also good with dried tagliatelle. This recipe shows how Italians like to eat their pasta sauce – just enough to coat the pasta, not a great big pile of sauce on top!

If you like the flavour of garlic, you could add a crushed glove of garlic with the onion in step two.

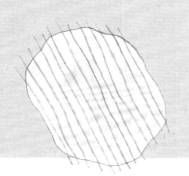

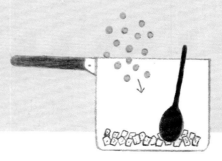

❶ If you are making fresh pasta, follow steps 1 to 7 on pages 40–41. Cut the pasta into long thin strips to make tagliatelle.

❷ Using the bridge and claw cutting techniques (see page 8), chop the onion or spring onions. Heat the butter and oil in a saucepan over a low heat (the butter adds flavour and the oil keeps it from burning). Add the onion and cook gently for 5 minutes until really soft. Stir every now and then with a wooden spoon.

❸ Add the peas, stir to coat them in the buttery juices and cook for 5 minutes, stirring every now and then with a wooden spoon. Using scissors, snip the ham into small pieces.

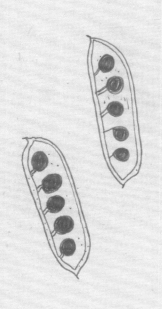

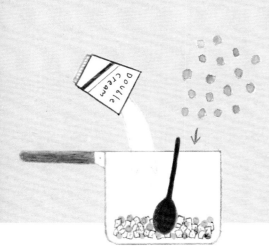

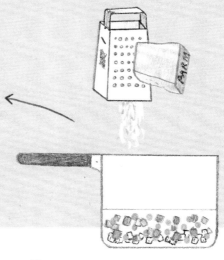

4 Add the cream and cook for another 5 minutes, then add the ham.

5 Three-quarters fill a large pan with water and bring to the boil. Add the fresh tagliatelle and cook for 3–4 minutes until the pasta is just cooked. It should be soft, and should not taste 'raw'. If you are using dried pasta, follow the instructions on page 39. Ask an adult to help you drain the pasta and put it back into the empty pan.

6 Ladle the sauce over the pasta. Grate the parmesan using the small holes on a grater (see page 9), and sprinkle over the pasta. Mix together and serve straight away!

Spaghetti with tomato sauce

Pomodoro
Golden apple

Makes enough for 4 people
- 400 g tin chopped tomatoes
- 1 teaspoon light brown soft sugar
- 1–2 garlic cloves, depending on how much you like the flavour of garlic
- 400 g spaghetti
- 10 fresh basil leaves
- 2 tablespoons olive oil

It's very hard to imagine Italian food without tomatoes, but in fact they have only been grown in Italy since the sixteenth century. At first, people were suspicious of tomatoes because they are related to a poisonous plant called deadly nightshade, but luckily for us, the Italians soon realised how delicious they were. The Italian name for tomato, pomodoro, means 'golden apple'.

❶ Put the tinned chopped tomatoes into a saucepan and add the sugar.

❷ Squash the cloves of garlic slightly with a rolling pin, then peel the garlic and add to the tomatoes.

❸ Bring the tomatoes up to a gentle simmer, cover and cook very gently over a very low heat for about 40 minutes. Stir the tomatoes occasionally with a wooden spoon.

Deadly nightshade

My poisonous
second cousins
←

4 When your sauce is nearly ready, bring a large pan of water to the boil and cook the spaghetti. See page 39 for how to cook pasta. Ask an adult to help you drain the spaghetti and put it back into the pan.

5 Take the tomato sauce off the heat, tear the basil leaves into small pieces and add to the sauce with the oil.

6 Carefully pour or ladle the sauce over the spaghetti, mix together and serve immediately.

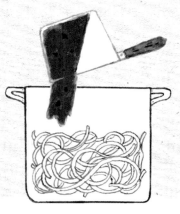

47

Spaghetti Amatriciana

Italians believe that each pasta shape should only be served with certain sauces. Long, thin pasta shapes are usually served with smooth sauces, but short, fat pasta shapes are often served with thicker ones because their holes can carry the pieces in the sauce. In this recipe, the spaghetti is coated in a tomato sauce. When you twist the spaghetti around your fork, you coat the pasta in its sauce and then eat both together.

1 The hottest parts of a chilli are the pithy white bit and the seeds, so if you take these out you will have the flavour of the chilli and a little heat but the sauce shouldn't be too hot. Using the bridge technique (see page 8) cut the chilli in half and then use a teaspoon to scrape out the seeds. If you touch the seeds, remember not to touch your eyes – the chilli juices will really make them sting! Using the claw technique cut the chilli into small pieces. Wash your hands straight away!

2 Using scissors (see page 7), snip the pancetta or bacon into small pieces, if it's not already cut into cubes.

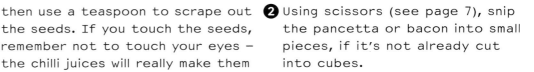

4 Put the olive oil into a heavy-based saucepan. Add the pancetta and cook over a medium heat for 3 minutes – the pancetta will change from bright pink to a paler pink as it starts to cook. Use a wooden spoon to stir the pancetta around in the pan.

5 Lower the heat, add the onion and cook very gently for 10 minutes, stirring every now and then – you want to cook the onions until they are soft.

6 Add the tinned tomatoes and chilli. Put the lid on the pan and leave over a gentle heat for 40 minutes. You will need to check it every 10 minutes and stir. Add a little more water if the sauce starts to stick to the bottom of the pan. The sauce will become thick and deep red in colour as it cooks.

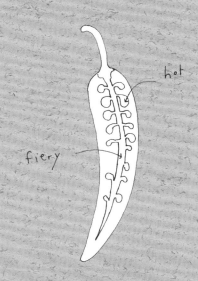

hot

fiery

3 Use the bridge and claw cutting techniques (see page 8) to chop the onion into small pieces.

7 When your sauce is nearly ready, bring a large pan of water to the boil and cook the spaghetti. See page 39 for how to cook pasta. Ask an adult to help you drain the spaghetti and put it back into the pan.

8 Taste the sauce and add freshly ground black pepper, ladle the sauce over the pasta and mix everything together. Serve immediately.

h o t

BURNING

F I R E

Linguine with pesto

Pesto is a bright green sauce from Liguria in northern Italy. Italians usually eat pesto with linguine or trofie pasta, which are little twisted rope shapes, but it's also delicious with steamed green beans or fresh gnocchi (see page 62). Traditionally, pesto is made with a pestle and mortar, which is perfect for pounding the ingredients — borrow one from a friend if you don't have one. You can also make it in a food processor.

Makes enough for 4 people
- 40 g Parmesan cheese or 20 g each of Parmesan and pecorino
- ½ clove garlic
- pinch of salt
- about 40 g pine nuts
- about 25 fresh basil leaves
- 3–4 tablespoons extra-virgin olive oil
- 400 g dried linguine pasta
- freshly ground black pepper

1 Finely grate the cheese (see page 9) and put to one side. Put the garlic and a small pinch of salt (this will make it easier to squash the garlic) into a mortar or food processor, and mash the garlic until it is soft and crushed.

2 Add the pine nuts and bash until they are broken into small pieces. If you're using a food processor it will only take seconds to whizz the nuts until they are broken into very small pieces, but if you're using a pestle and mortar you might need to take it in turns with friends or family to help you bash everything, to stop your arm from aching!

3 Add the basil leaves and mash some more. If you're using a pestle and mortar, bash the leaves until they are broken into small pieces. Try to do this quite quickly, to keep the bright green colour – the longer you bash, the darker the leaves will go. If you're using a food processor, blend quickly in short bursts.

4 Spoon the mixture into a bowl, add the cheese and mix. Then gradually add the oil, until you have a sauce that just drops off your spoon. Hey presto, you've made pesto!

SMash!

Pummel

Pound

CRush

BASH!

some bashing

more bashing

even more bashing

⑤ Bring a large pan of water to the boil and cook the linguine. See page 39 for how to cook pasta. You will need to ask an adult to help you drain the linguine and tip it back into the empty pan. Add the pesto and carefully stir to coat the pasta with the pesto. Season with freshly ground black pepper, and eat!

Baked Macaroni with Parmesan

Makes enough for 4 people

For the béchamel sauce:
- 50 g unsalted butter
- 50 g plain flour
- 600 ml full-fat milk
- freshly ground black pepper

For the baked macaroni:
- 300 g macaroni pasta
- 30 g Parmesan cheese
- 30 g Cheddar cheese

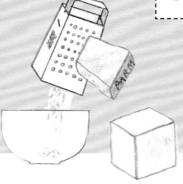

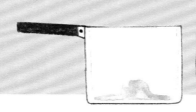

❶ Start by grating the Parmesan and Cheddar cheeses carefully, making sure that your fingers stay well away from the grater (see page 9). Set these aside as you will use them later in the recipe.

❷ Now make the sauce. Put the butter in a small pan and melt over a gentle heat. You don't want to overheat the butter or let it brown, as this will affect the colour and flavour of the sauce.

❸ As soon as the butter has melted, add the flour and cook the mixture over a medium heat for 1 minute, stirring constantly with a wooden spoon to make a smooth glossy paste – this is your roux.

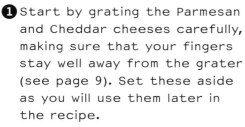

❼ Keep the pan on a low heat and let the sauce cook very gently for 3–4 minutes, stirring constantly. The sauce will continue to thicken as it cooks. You'll know it's ready when the sauce is thick enough to coat the back of your wooden spoon.

❽ Turn the oven on to 200°C/400°F/ Gas Mark 6. Then bring a large pan of water to the boil and cook the macaroni. See page 39 for how to cook pasta. You will need to ask an adult to help you drain the macaroni and tip it back into the empty pan.

❾ Add the Parmesan and Cheddar to the béchamel sauce and season with a little freshly ground black pepper.

To make baked macaroni, you first have to make a very useful white sauce called <u>béchamel</u> (pronounced 'bay-sha-mel'). To make it, you start by cooking a combination of butter and flour known as a <u>roux</u> (pronounced 'roo'). Once you have learnt how to make béchamel sauce, you can use it in many other dishes, like lasagne (see page 54). This sauce tastes quite plain to start with, so in this recipe, flavour is added with cheese.

4 Take off the heat, add about 4 tablespoons of the milk, and stir until the milk is completely mixed in. The mixture will go very thick, so stir until it is smooth.

5 Put back on a low heat, add a little more milk and stir again. Continue to add milk a little at a time until you have added half of the milk.

6 Swap your wooden spoon for a whisk and continue to add the rest of the milk. You can add more at a time now, as long as you keep whisking to help prevent the sauce from going lumpy!

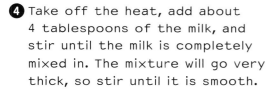

10 Ladle, spoon or pour half of the béchamel sauce over the pasta and use a wooden spoon to mix the pasta and sauce together.

11 Spoon the pasta into an ovenproof dish about 25 cm square (or you can can use any ovenproof dish you have). Spoon the remaining béchamel sauce over the top of the pasta. If you have a ladle, you might find it easier to use this.

12 Put the ovenproof dish onto a baking tray. Wearing your oven gloves, put it into the oven and cook for 20 minutes until it is golden brown and bubbling. Serve with salad or cooked green vegetables.

Lasagne

Lasagne is made up of layers of pasta, béchamel sauce and a meat-based sauce (called ragù in Italian). The lasagne that Italian children eat is slightly different from what you might be used to – they expect a slice of lasagne to stand up on the plate and hold its shape. This recipe shows you how to make lasagne the Italian way.

Makes enough for 4 people

For the ragù:
– 1 carrot
– 1 onion
– 1 clove garlic
– 2 tablespoons olive oil
– 350g good quality minced beef
– 100ml water
– 500g tomato passata

– 1 quantity béchamel sauce (see page 52)
– about 12 sheets lasagne pasta*
– 40g Parmesan cheese

* You can make fresh pasta for this if you like (see page 40), or you can buy dried lasagne pasta sheets that are ready to use

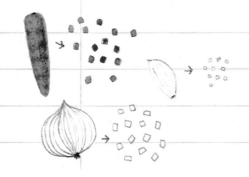

❶ To make the ragù, start by finely chopping the carrot and onion using the bridge and claw techniques (see page 8), and crush the garlic with a garlic crusher (see page 7).

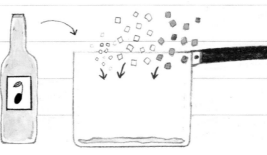

❷ Put the oil, carrot, onion and garlic in a pan, and cook over a low heat for about 10 minutes until really soft, stirring every now and then.

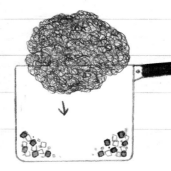

❸ Push the vegetables to the side of the pan and add the beef, making sure it covers the base of the pan. Leave it to cook until it has turned brown (3–4 minutes). Stir everything together and cook for another 3–4 minutes. Stir every now and then to cook the meat and the vegetables evenly.

❺ Turn the oven on to 180°C/350°F/Gas Mark 4. You will need an ovenproof dish about 25cm × 20cm big. Spread a little ragù over the base of the dish, then spread a little béchamel sauce over the top.

Each layer of sauce should be quite thin, like a layer of jam on toast. Then rest a layer of pasta sheets over the top. Keep layering the ragù, the béchamel sauce and then the pasta.

❻ For this size dish, you should have 4 layers of pasta (3 sheets in each layer). Finish the lasagne with a layer of pasta topped with béchamel sauce. Sprinkle a little grated Parmesan over the top of the lasagne.

Lasagne Geology

Key

Béchamel
Lasagne
Ragù

ITALY

Mediterranean Sea

4 Add the water and the passata and simmer gently (the mixture will be just very gently bubbling) for 30 minutes. You can also add a sprig of fresh rosemary or sage or a bay leaf to the ragù for extra flavour if you like. Make the béchamel sauce if you haven't already, and grate the Parmesan cheese (see page 9).

7 Put the dish on a baking tray. Using oven gloves, put the tray in the oven and bake for 35 minutes until golden and bubbling. Serve with salad or green vegetables.

Rigatoni with Meatballs

Makes enough for 4 people
- handful of fresh flat-leaf parsley
- ½ garlic clove
- 400 g minced beef or 200 g each of minced pork and minced beef
- freshly ground black pepper
- 1 free-range egg
- handful of plain flour, for dusting
- 1 onion
- 1 celery stick
- 1 carrot
- 2 tablespoons olive oil
- 1 small sprig fresh rosemary
- 500 ml tomato passata
- 400 g rigatoni pasta
- 25 g Parmesan cheese

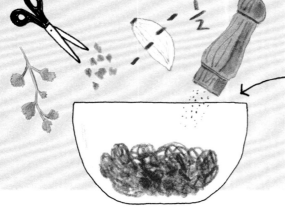

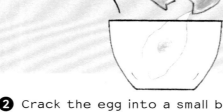

❶ Using scissors (see page 7), snip the parsley leaves into small pieces. Crush the garlic (see page 7). Put the minced meat into a large bowl, add the parsley and garlic and season with some freshly ground black pepper.

❷ Crack the egg into a small bowl (see page 9), and add it to the meat.

❸ Put your hands into the mixture and mix everything together – you can use a fork if you prefer but it's more fun with your hands.

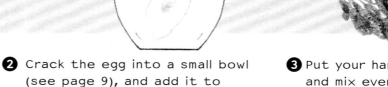

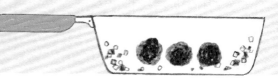

❼ Using the bridge and claw cutting techniques (see page 8), chop the onion, celery and carrot into small pieces.

❽ Put the oil into a heavy-based pan, add the onion, carrot and celery and cook over a low heat for 10 minutes, stirring every now and then with a wooden spoon.

❾ Push the carrot mixture to the sides of the pan, add the meatballs and cook for another 5 minutes without moving the meatballs.

Making meatballs is a great way to practise your maths and learn about fractions: in this recipe, you have to divide the mixture for the meatballs into eight equal pieces. It's good to make all the meatballs the same size, so that they will cook evenly. Rigatoni is a type of tube-shaped pasta with ridges around the outside, but you could use penne or any other short types of pasta instead.

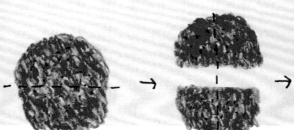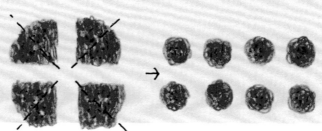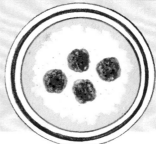

4 Divide the mixture in half, then into quarters and then into eighths.

5 Using your hands shape the mixture into 8 balls.

6 Sprinkle the flour onto a plate and then dip each meatball into the flour. Put the meatballs on a plate and into the fridge.

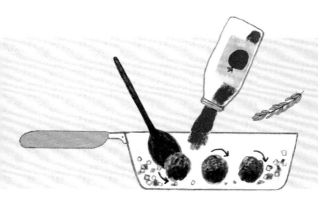

10 Very carefully turn the meatballs over in the pan so that they brown, making sure they don't fall apart. Add the rosemary and passata and continue to cook gently over a low heat for about 40 minutes, until the meatballs are cooked through.

11 Bring a large pan of water to the boil and cook the rigatoni. See page 39 for how to cook pasta.

12 Divide the pasta among your serving bowls and ladle the meatballs on top. Make sure you throw away the rosemary stalk! Grate the Parmesan (see page 9) and sprinkle over the top.

Main
Courses

Risotto

Risotto is a dish from northern Italy made with rice and stock (a liquid flavoured with ingredients such as vegetables or chicken). In Milan, risotto is made with saffron, which adds a beautiful golden colour.

The most important ingredient is good quality risotto rice, ideally carnaroli or vialone nano, both of which are available from good food shops. When cooked, this rice has a firm texture as well as a creamy softness. This may be hard to imagine, but when you have cooked a good risotto, you'll see what I mean. Once you know how to make a basic risotto, you can add other ingredients, like vegetables or meat.

<u>Makes enough for 4 people</u>
- 40–50 g Parmesan cheese
- 1.2–1.4 litres vegetable or chicken stock (if you are not using fresh stock, use a good vegetable stock powder)
- 1 onion
- 40 g unsalted butter
- 1 tablespoon olive oil
- 350 g risotto rice
- ½ teaspoon saffron threads

Soffritto

❶ Carefully grate the Parmesan cheese (see page 9) and put to one side. Pour the stock into a saucepan and bring up to simmering point – this is when it is very gently bubbling. Get a ladle and put it by the pan, ready for later.

❷ Using the bridge and claw cutting techniques (see page 8), chop the onion. Melt half the butter and oil in a heavy-based pan (the butter adds flavour and the oil keeps it from burning). Add the onion and cook gently for 10 minutes until it is really soft, occasionally stirring with a wooden spoon. This stage is known in Italy as the 'soffritto', and it forms the base of the risotto. If you are making a different flavoured risotto, you would add your other ingredients, such as garlic or mushrooms or sausage meat, at this stage.

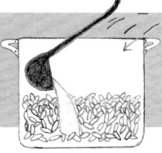

18 - 20

bite

soft and creamy

❹ Carefully add a couple of ladles of stock and the saffron threads and stir gently until the liquid has been absorbed by the rice. Then add another couple of ladles of hot stock and cook, still stirring, until it has been absorbed.

❺ Keep adding the stock in this way until it has all been used up – only add more stock when the liquid in the pan has been absorbed. It should take about 18–20 minutes until the rice is cooked and all the stock has been absorbed.

Take a small spoon and taste the rice to see if it is ready – it should be soft but still have some 'bite', but it will also taste slightly creamy.

tostatura

3 The next stage is known as the 'tostatura', or the toasting of the rice. Add the rice to the pan and stir to coat it thoroughly with the onion and butter.

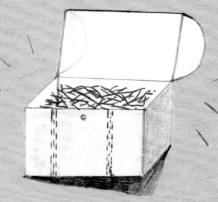

Saffron is made from crocus flowers, and takes a lot of work to produce: Italian saffron growers say that a gram of saffron is more valuable than a gram of gold.

Mantecatura

6 Lower the heat and add the remaining butter and the grated Parmesan cheese and stir — this stage is called the 'mantecatura', and it helps to give the risotto its lovely texture. Serve immediately.

Potato Gnocchi

Makes enough for 4 people
- 1kg potatoes
- 1 large free-range egg
- 240g plain flour

Gnocchi (pronounced 'nee-ockee') are little dumplings that can be made from potatoes, flour or cornmeal. Many regions of Italy have their own special types of gnocchi. They are easy to make and great fun to shape! Gnocchi can be eaten with different sauces, like the pesto on page 50, or the tomato sauce on page 46.

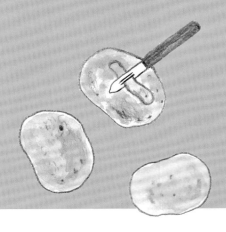

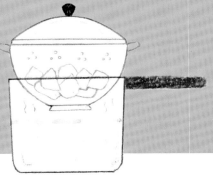

❶ Using a vegetable peeler, peel the potatoes (see page 9).

❷ Using the bridge technique (see page 8) cut each potato in half. Then rest the halves cut side down on a board before you cut them into quarters. Put the potatoes into a colander.

❸ Half-fill a saucepan with water and put the colander on top. Cover with a lid, bring up to the boil, and steam the potatoes for 20 minutes. Cooked like this, the potatoes don't absorb too much water – you want them to be quite dry to make the gnocchi.

❼ Sprinkle some flour over your work surface, and put the dough onto the flour. Shape the dough into a big square. It should be about 1.5 cm thick. Using a table knife, cut the square in half. Cut each half of dough into thin strips – about 1.5 cm wide.

❽ Roll each strip into a long thin sausage shape with your hands. Then cut them into small pieces about 1.5 cm long, so you end up with lots of small cylindrical pieces. It doesn't matter if the pieces of dough are slightly different shapes, but you do want them to be quite even in size so that they take the same amount of time to cook.

❾ In Italy, gnocchi traditionally has a pattern on it. You can make this pattern by pushing the gnocchi against a grater or the tines of a fork, but you don't have to.
Sprinkle some flour over a big plate or baking tray and put the gnocchi on the flour.

4 Turn off the hob. Ask an adult to help you take the colander off the pan. Carefully poke a skewer or fork into a potato to see if it is cooked – the skewer should glide easily into the potato.

5 Put the potatoes into a bowl and using a potato masher or a ricer mash until smooth. A potato ricer looks like a very big garlic crusher, and works in the same way. Leave to cool.

6 Crack the egg into a bowl (see page 9). Add the flour and egg to the cooled mashed potato and mix with a wooden spoon. Then put your hands into the bowl and mix to make a dough.

The gnocchi go for a quick dip in boiling water

DEEP WATER

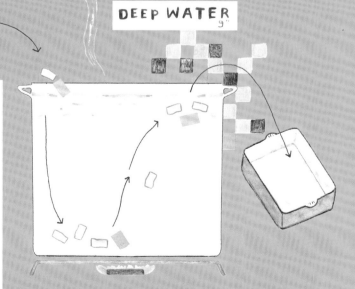

10 Heat a serving dish in a low oven so you can keep your gnocchi warm when they are cooked. Ask an adult to help you bring a large pan of water to the boil, add about 8 pieces of gnocchi, and wait for the gnocchi to rise to the surface of the water. They are cooked when they come up to the top – this will only take about 1 minute.

11 Using a slotted spoon lift the gnocchi out of the pan and put into your warm serving dish. Cook the rest of the gnocchi. Ladle your sauce on top, and it's readly to eat!

Polenta gnocchi

Polenta is a type of coarse flour made from corn. It looks like a thick yellow porridge while it's cooking. It needs a lot of stirring, but then it sets into a solid slab that you can cut out into different shapes. It's delicious served with melted butter and cheese, which is how the Italians often eat it.

Makes enough for 4 people
- a little olive oil for brushing the tray
- 350 g coarse polenta flour
- 20 g unsalted butter
- 40 g Parmesan cheese

❶ You will need a baking tray that is about 20 cm × 30 cm big. Brush a little oil over your baking tray.

❺ Carefully spoon the polenta mixture onto the baking tray. You might like to use a ladle to do this. Spread out the polenta to make an even rectangle and leave to cool and set.

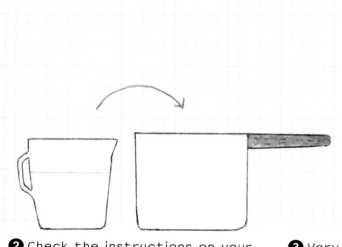

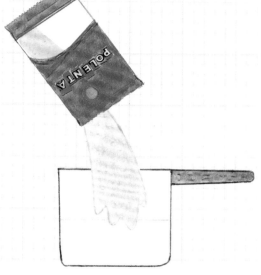

2 Check the instructions on your packet of polenta. Most polenta flours are similar, but it is always worth checking! You will need to measure out the water as directed on the packet, pour it into a big saucepan and bring it to the boil.

3 Very carefully pour the polenta flour into the water – you may need to ask an adult to help you do this. You will need to stir the polenta flour in the water with a wooden spoon to make sure that it doesn't go lumpy.

4 Lower the heat and cook gently, and keep stirring all the time until the polenta is thick and smooth. This will take about 3 minutes, or the length of time suggested on the packet.

6 When the polenta is cold, stamp out the rounds using a glass – dip the edge of the glass in water to stop the polenta from sticking to it. You could also use a biscuit cutter (about 6 cm in diameter). Start cutting the circles along one edge of the polenta to make sure that you can cut out as many as possible.

7 Turn the oven on to 180 °C⁄ 350 ° F⁄Gas Mark 4. Brush a little oil over a wide baking sheet. Arrange a circle of the polenta rounds on the tray. Top with another smaller layer of polenta rounds and keep layering the rounds until you have a flat pyramid shape. You could make one big pyramid or two small ones.

8 Grate the Parmesan carefully (see page 9), making sure your fingers stay well away from the grater. Sprinkle the Parmesan over the polenta stacks and dot with butter. Wearing your oven gloves, put in the oven and bake for 20 minutes until golden brown. Serve with cooked green vegetables, like beans or broccoli.

Baked Aubergine with tomato

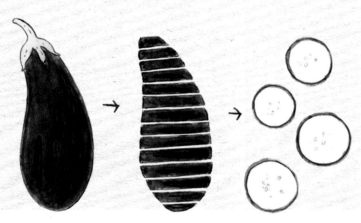  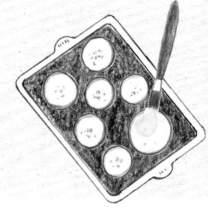

1 Turn the oven on to 200°C/400°F/ Gas Mark 6. Using the claw cutting technique (see page 8), slice the aubergines into rounds. Make the slices about 5 mm thick if you can – they can be a bit thicker if you find that easier.

2 Brush a roasting dish with a tablespoon of olive oil and arrange the aubergine slices over the dish in one single layer, so that they are not overlapping each other.

Brush the slices with another tablespoon of oil. Wearing your oven gloves, put the tray into the oven and roast for 20 minutes until soft and slightly golden.

  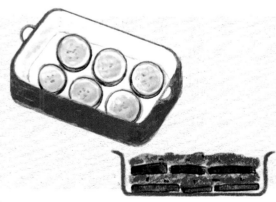

3 Meanwhile, using the bridge and claw techniques (see page 8), chop the onions. Crush the garlic using a garlic crusher (see page 7). Put the rest of the olive oil in a saucepan, add the onion and garlic and cook gently over a low heat for 5 minutes, stirring every now and then with a wooden spoon.

4 Add the chopped tomatoes to the pan. Using scissors (see page 7), snip the parsley into small pieces and add to the pan. Simmer gently for about 15 minutes until the sauce has thickened.

5 Arrange a layer of aubergine slices in the bottom of an ovenproof dish, ladle or spoon half the tomato sauce over the top, cover with another layer of aubergine slices and then top with another layer of tomato sauce.

Aubergines have beautiful purple shiny skins, and they are delicious cooked in this way with tomatoes and cheese. This recipe is fantastic on its own with bread and salad, or served alongside a main course such as roast chicken or lamb.

<u>Makes enough for 4 people</u>
- 2 aubergines
- 3 tablespoons olive oil
- 2 onions
- 2 cloves garlic
- 400 g tin chopped tomatoes
- 1 sprig fresh flat-leaf parsley
- 80 g Emmenthal cheese
- 50 g breadcrumbs
- a small piece unsalted butter

6 Grate the cheese carefully into a small bowl, making sure that your fingers stay well away from the grater (see page 9). Add the breadcrumbs, mix together and sprinkle over the top of the aubergine.

7 Put the dish onto a baking tray and dot with butter. Wearing your oven gloves, put the tray in the oven and bake for 20 minutes until golden. Serve hot.

serve with bread and salad

Beans with Sausages

❶ Turn on the oven to 190°C/375°F/ Gas Mark 5. Prick the sausages all over with a fork. Put into a heavy-based roasting dish, add the whole garlic cloves with the skin left on and the olive oil. Using oven gloves, put into the oven for 20 minutes. The sausages will turn lovely and brown as they cook in the roasting dish – this will help colour the beans and the gravy juice later.

❷ Put your oven gloves on and take the roasting dish out of the oven. Using tongs or a knife and fork, carefully turn the sausages over. The sausages will then go brown on the other side when they go back in the oven.

Beans and sausages are a classic combination, simple and delicious. In this recipe, you pour some apple juice in with the beans, which may sound a bit strange at first, but it makes for a really wonderful sweet sauce for the beans!

<u>Makes enough for 4 people</u>
- 8–12 good quality pork sausages (depending on how many you want to eat!)
- 2 cloves garlic
- 2 teaspoons olive oil
- 2 fresh sage leaves
- 400 g tin cannellini beans, rinsed and drained
- 100 ml apple juice
- freshly ground black pepper

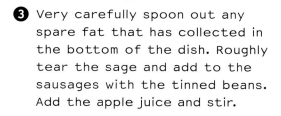

❸ Very carefully spoon out any spare fat that has collected in the bottom of the dish. Roughly tear the sage and add to the sausages with the tinned beans. Add the apple juice and stir.

❹ Wearing your oven gloves, put back into the oven for another 20 minutes until the beans are hot and slightly soft. Carefully stir everything with a wooden spoon, and add a little freshly ground black pepper. Serve with some fresh cooked green vegetables. If you like, you can serve the beans and sausages in a pretty dish, but it's not necessary!

Baked Cod with Vegetables

This dish looks good and tastes great, with the colourful vegetables sitting under the white cod wrapped in the pink pancetta. Any firm white fish, such as hake, gurnard or haddock, will be equally delicious in this recipe.

<u>Makes enough for 4 people</u>
- 1 small leek or ½ big leek
- 2 carrots
- 200 g tin chopped tomatoes
- 20 g unsalted butter
- 1 tablespoon olive oil
- 4 cod fillets, or any other firm white fish, skin removed
- 1 lemon
- 8 slices pancetta

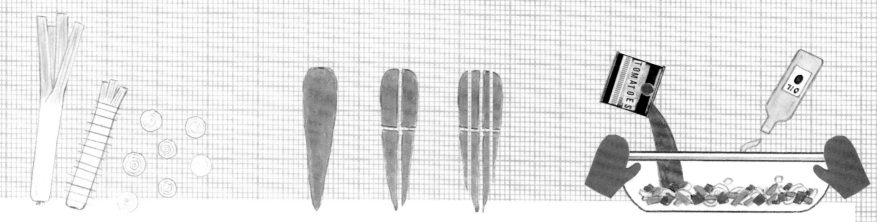

1 Turn the oven on to 190°C/ 375°F/Gas Mark 5. Wash the leek and, using the bridge cutting technique (see page 8), trim off the roots and dark green leaves. Using the claw technique (see page 8), cut the leek into slices, as thinly as possible.

2 Wash and peel the carrots. Using the bridge technique, trim the tips off the top and bottom of the carrot, then slice it in half widthways and then in half lengthways. Rest the flat sides of the carrot on a board and cut into into thin slices using the claw technique.

3 Put the tomatoes, leek and carrots into a heavy-based roasting tin, dot with the butter and drizzle with the oil. Wearing your oven gloves, put the tin in the oven and roast for 20 minutes.

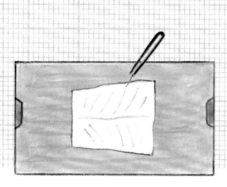 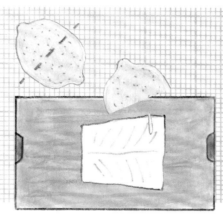 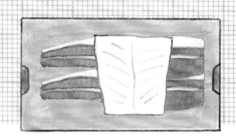

4 While the vegetables are cooking, put the fish fillets onto a chopping board and check for any bones. Carefully run your fingers over the pieces of fish and if you feel a bone, pull it out with tweezers.

5 Using the bridge technique, cut the lemon in half. Squeeze the lemon juice over the fish, and brush any lemon pips to the side so you can throw them away.

6 Put 2 slices of pancetta onto the board, put a cod fillet onto the pancetta and then wrap the pancetta around the fish. Repeat with the other fillets.

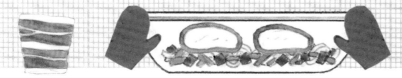

7 When the vegetables have cooked for 20 minutes, using your oven gloves, take the roasting tin out of the oven. Carefully put the fish on top of the vegetables, with the pancetta 'seam' facing downwards.

Using your oven gloves, put the roasting tin back in the oven and cook for another 10–15 minutes. Then cut one of the fillets in half to check that it is cooked: the fish should be white and opaque

instead of slightly transparent. If it is not cooked all the way through, cook for another 5 minutes.

Fish Kebabs

Makes 8 kebabs
You will need 8 wooden skewers
- 800g fresh fish, for example tilapia, gurnard, whiting, pollack, salmon, haddock and cod
- 8 big raw prawns, peeled
- handful of small mushrooms
- handful of cherry tomatoes
- handful of stoned olives

For the marinade:
- 1 clove garlic
- ½ lemon
- 2 tablespoons olive oil
- small handful fresh flat-leaf parsley leaves

This recipe calls for a variety of different types of fish, so ask your fishmonger for a selection of fresh fish for fish kebabs. You'll notice when you buy them that raw prawns are grey – they only turn pink when they are cooked!

If you buy prawns with their shells, you'll need to peel them before making the kebabs. These kebabs are also great cooked on a barbecue

❶ Turn the oven on to 190°C/ 375°F/Gas Mark 5. Put the pieces of fish onto a chopping board, remove any skin and run your fingers over them checking for bones. Use tweezers to pull out any bones you find.

❷ Using the bridge technique (see page 8), cut the fish into big chunks – about 2.5cm square. If you cut the fish too small, it is more likely to fall off the skewers.

❸ To make the marinade, peel and crush the garlic and put into a bowl. Squeeze the lemon juice onto the garlic. Add the oil and mix together. Using scissors, snip the parsley leaves and add to the oil mixture. Mix everything together with a spoon. See page 7 to remind yourself how to do these things!

4 Hold a piece of fish between your thumb and finger and push a skewer though the middle of the fish. Carry on pushing pieces of fish onto the skewer, alternating the different types of fish with prawns, mushrooms, tomatoes and olives. You can make up your own special sequence, so that you know which one is yours when the kebabs come out of the oven!

5 Put the kebabs into a large ovenproof dish, pour the marinade over the fish and carefully move the kebabs around to make sure that they are covered with the marinade. Leave to marinate in the refrigerator for about 20 minutes.

6 Put your oven gloves on, put the fish into the oven and cook for 10 minutes. Take out of the oven and, using oven gloves or tongs, turn the skewers over. Wearing your oven gloves, put back into the oven and cook for another 5 minutes or until cooked. Serve hot.

Chicken stew with Olives

Makes enough for 4 people
- 4 large pieces or 8 small pieces of chicken, such as legs or thighs
- 15 g unsalted butter
- 1 tablespoon olive oil
- 150 g black olives
- 400 g tin chopped tomatoes
- 1 teaspoon light brown soft sugar
- 1 sprig fresh parsley
- 4 fresh basil leaves

Olives are green or black. They grow on trees, and the green olives are picked quite early, when they are still young. The black ones are picked later, when they are riper. They are often softer and have a milder flavour. You can use any pieces of chicken you like for this recipe, such as thighs or legs. Serve this stew with polenta, bread, pasta, rice or potatoes. This is a tasty, simple dish — with just a few basic ingredients, you can make a classic Italian meal!

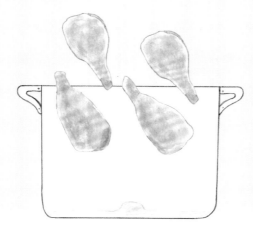

❶ Turn the oven on to 170°C/325°F/Gas Mark 3. Pull the skin away from the pieces of chicken. Put the butter and oil in a heavy-based flameproof casserole dish, heat on a hob until the butter has melted, add the chicken pieces and cook over a medium heat for 5 minutes without touching the chicken.

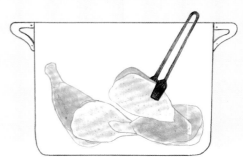

❷ Using tongs, turn the chicken pieces over — they should be a nice golden colour on one side. Cook for another 3 minutes. Take off the heat.

young olives

older olives

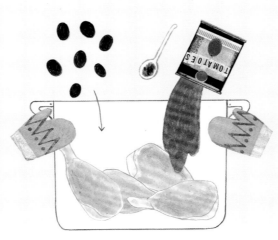

3 Using a rolling pin, carefully squash an olive slightly so you can open it up and take the stone out. Do this with all the olives.

4 Pour the tinned tomatoes over the chicken, fill the empty can with water and add to the chicken with the olives and sugar. Stir with a wooden spoon, cover with a lid and, using oven gloves, put in the oven and cook for 40 minutes.

5 Wearing your oven gloves, take the casserole dish out of the oven. Tear the basil and use scissors (see page 7) to snip the parsley. Sprinkle the herbs over the top and serve with polenta, bread, pasta, rice or potatoes.

Chicken breasts stuffed with Mascarpone

Mascarpone is a rich creamy cheese, which can be used in both savoury and sweet dishes. Serve these stuffed chicken breasts with fresh steamed vegetables, like broccoli or green beans, and potatoes or rice.

Makes enough for 4 people
- 125 g mushrooms (any type will do)
- 1 clove garlic
- handful fresh flat-leaf parsley leaves
- 1 teaspoon olive oil
- 20 g unsalted butter
- 4 skinless, boneless chicken breast portions
- 100 g mascarpone cheese
- 4 slices prosciutto (see page 12) or Parma ham
- freshly ground black pepper

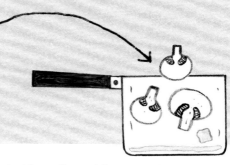

❶ Turn the oven on to 200°C/ 400°F/ Gas Mark 6. Using the bridge cutting technique (see page 8) chop the mushrooms in half and then using the claw technique (see page 8) slice as thinly as possible.

❷ Peel the papery skin away from the garlic clove and crush the garlic with a garlic crusher. Snip the parsley leaves with scissors (see page 7).

❸ Put the oil and butter into a small saucepan, add the garlic, mushrooms and parsley and cook over a low heat for 5 minutes until the mushrooms are soft.

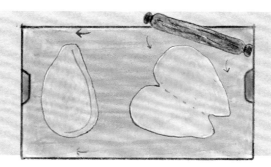

❹ Add a little freshly ground black pepper. Spoon the mushrooms into a bowl and leave until the mixture is really cool. This is important, as you don't want to put hot mixture in the uncooked chicken breasts.

❺ Ask an adult to help you cut a slit in the chicken. Put a piece of chicken on a chopping board. Holding your hand flat on top of the chicken fillet, very carefully slice into the side of the chicken without cutting all the way through, then open the piece of chicken like a book. Cover the chicken with a piece of clingfilm. Using a rolling pin, carefully bash the chicken fillet – you want to flatten it slightly so that it cooks quickly in the oven and stays moist. Do the same with the other pieces of chicken. Don't forget to wash the rolling pin carefully after you have used it to flatten the chicken!

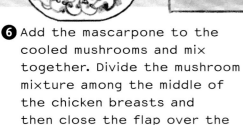

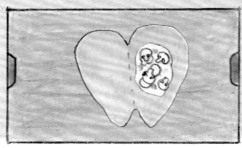

❻ Add the mascarpone to the cooled mushrooms and mix together. Divide the mushroom mixture among the middle of the chicken breasts and then close the flap over the mascarpone mixture.

❼ Wrap a slice of prosciutto around the chicken and put the chicken wrapped in ham onto a roasting tray, with the 'seam' facing downwards.

❽ Wearing your oven gloves, put the tray into the oven and roast for 20 minutes. Cut one chicken breast in half to check that it is cooked all the way through. If it is at all pink, put it back in the oven for another 5 minutes or until it's well cooked.

Beef Stew

Makes enough for 4 people

<u>Makes enough for 4 people</u>
- 150 g pancetta or bacon bits
- 1 onion
- 1 celery stick
- 1 carrot
- 1 tablespoon olive oil
- 600 g lean stewing steak (ask your butcher to cut the beef into small chunks for you)
- 400 g tin chopped tomatoes
- 1 teaspoon light brown soft sugar
- 1 sprig rosemary
- 400 ml vegetable stock (if you are not using fresh stock, use a good vegetable stock powder)
- freshly ground black pepper

It's really useful to learn how to make a stew. Not only does it taste great, it's all cooked in one pan, so there's not much washing up! And once it's in the oven, you can go off and do something else while it cooks. Serve this stew with mashed potatoes or new potatoes with rosemary (see page 80).

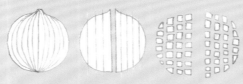

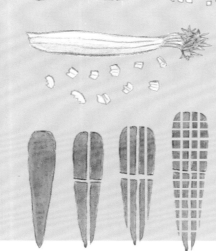

1 Turn the oven on to 150°C/300°F/Gas Mark 2. If your pancetta or bacon is not already cubed, use the bridge technique (see page 8) to cut the slices into small pieces – first into thin strips and then into small cubes.

2 Using the bridge and claw cutting techniques (see page 8), chop the onion, celery and carrot into small pieces.

3 Put the oil in a heavy-based flameproof casserole dish and add the pancetta, onion, celery and carrot and cook gently over a low heat for 10 minutes. Stir occasionally with a wooden spoon.

4 Push the vegetables to the sides of the pan, add the meat and cook until just brown – this will take about 5 minutes. If you prefer, you can spoon the vegetables out of the pan onto a plate so you can cook the meat in the empty pan, and then put the vegetables back afterwards.

5 Add the tomatoes, sugar and rosemary. Fill the empty tomato tin with stock and add to the pan – this helps to make sure that you use all the tomato juices in the tin. Add any leftover stock to the pan.

6 Stir everything together with a wooden spoon. Wearing your oven gloves, put the pan into the oven and cook very gently for 2 hours. You might need to ask an adult to check if the oven temperature needs to be lowered. Season with freshly ground black pepper before serving.

Lamb Chops and new potatoes with rosemary

Lamb is reallly tasty when it's cooked with fresh herbs such as mint. In Italy, it is almost always cooked with herbs. This recipe uses a marinade – this mixture of lemon juice, oil and herbs helps to make the lamb more tender and flavoursome.

Makes enough for 4 people
- 1 lemon
- 1 sprig fresh mint
- 2 tablespoons olive oil
- 4 lamb chops

For the roasted new potatoes:
- 675 g new potatoes
- 1 sprig fresh rosemary
- 1 garlic clove
- 2 tablespoons olive oil

❶ Using the bridge technique (see page 8), cut the lemon in half and then squeeze its juice into a bowl (see page 9). Pull the mint leaves off the stalk and add to the lemon juice with the oil and mix everything together.

❷ Put the lamb chops into the lemon juice mixture and mix to make sure that the meat is well coated in the oil.

❸ Leave to marinate for 1 hour. This gives the chops time to absorb all those lovely oil and herb flavours – you will find that the lamb is really tender and has wonderful flavour when it is cooked.

4 Once the lamb has been marinating for 45 minutes, turn the oven on to 190°C/375°F/Gas Mark 5. Using the bridge technique, cut the potatoes in half lengthways and put into a roasting tin with the rosemary and garlic. Drizzle over the oil and, using oven gloves, put the tin in the oven and roast for 20 minutes.

5 Take the lamb out of the marinade and if your pan is big enough, add the lamb to the potatoes. If not, you will need another roasting dish for the lamb. Roast the lamb chops for 10 minutes. Wearing your oven gloves, take the lamb out of the oven and, using tongs, turn the chops over.

6 Using oven gloves, put the dish back into the oven for another 10 minutes. The potatoes should be golden and tender when you poke them with a skewer or table knife. The lamb will be very slightly pink in the middle, which is how it should be. Cook for a little bit longer if you prefer.

Roast leg of lamb in a herb crust with stuffed tomatoes

This is a great dish for a big family dinner or celebration. It goes really well with the stuffed tomatoes included in this recipe, but you could also eat it with broccoli or green beans. You can try other herb combinations: fresh mint instead of thyme also tastes good. The cooking times given in this recipe will mean that the lamb is slightly pink in the middle, so cook it for 10 minutes longer if you prefer.

Makes enough for 6 people
- 1 sprig fresh thyme or mint
- 1 sprig fresh oregano
  or 2 teaspoons dried oregano
- 1 sprig fresh flat-leaf parsley
- 1 sprig fresh rosemary
- 1 slice toasted bread, white
  or brown
- 2 tablespoons olive oil
- 1.3 kg leg of lamb

For the stuffed tomatoes:
- 4 ripe tomatoes
- 2 slices toasted bread, white
  or brown
- a few fresh oregano leaves
- 1 tablespoon olive oil

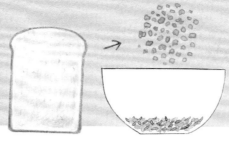

❶ Turn the oven on to 200°C/400°F/ Gas Mark 6. Pull the herb leaves off the stalks, then using scissors (see page 7), snip the leaves into small pieces and put into a bowl.

❷ Crumble the piece of toast into breadcrumbs using your fingers. Add to the bowl of herbs.

❸ Add the oil to the herbs and breadcrumbs, and mix well.

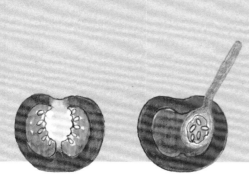

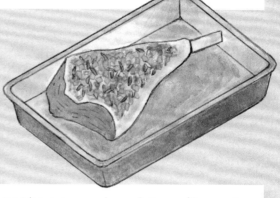

❹ Put the leg of lamb into a big roasting tin and use your hands to spread the herb mixture all over the meat. Add 150 ml water to the roasting tin. Using oven gloves, put the tin into the oven and roast for 15 minutes.

❺ Lower the oven temperature to 180°C/350°F/Gas Mark 4 and roast for another 35 minutes. These timings are correct for a 1.3 kg leg of lamb, so if yours is a different weight, you will need to put some maths to good use! You will need to cook the lamb for 20 minutes per 500 g, plus another 20 minutes. Or to put it another way, for 4 minutes for every 100 g of lamb plus 20 minutes.

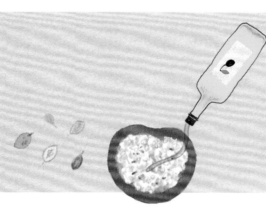

❻ In the meantime, cut the tomatoes in half using the bridge technique (see page 8). Scoop out the seeds with a teaspoon. Crumble the other 2 pieces of toast with your fingers and spoon into the tomatoes. Sprinkle over the oregano and drizzle over the oil.

❼ When the lamb has been in the oven for 35 minutes, ask an adult to help you take the roasting tin out of the oven. Add the tomatoes to the tin and put back in the oven. Or you can put the tomatoes into an ovenproof dish and using oven gloves, put it into the oven next to the roasting tin.

❽ Roast the tomatoes and lamb for another 25 minutes. Using your oven gloves, take the lamb out of the oven and leave it to rest for 5 minutes before serving.

CAKE

self-raising flour

Vanilla

teaspoon

dessertspoon

tablespoon

SUGAR

Desserts and Baking

Focaccia

Focaccia is a type of flat bread that is really popular in Italy. It has dimples all over to hold the delicious flavours of olive oil and rosemary, and is very easy to make. Once you've made this version, you could try adding other flavours on top, such as grated cheese, sun-dried tomatoes or olives.

Makes one big loaf
- 3–4 tablespoons olive oil plus extra for brushing the tray
- 500 g strong bread flour, plus extra for dusting
- 7 g sachet dried active yeast

For the topping:
- 2 tablespoons olive oil
- handful fresh rosemary leaves, or another topping of your choice

❶ Start by pouring 125 ml cold water into your measuring jug and then add enough hot water to make 250 ml. Dip your finger in to test the temperature – it should just feel warm.

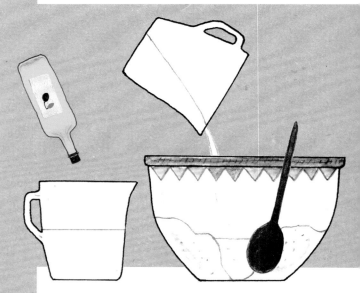

❺ Add the oil to the water and pour the warm water into the well. Use a wooden spoon to mix to a soft dough.

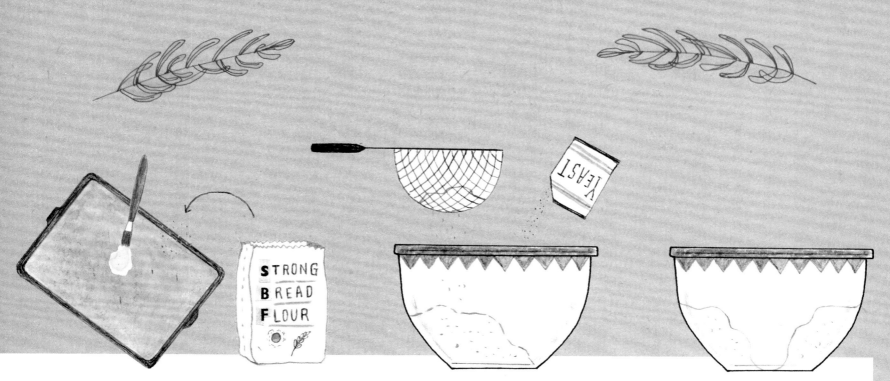

2 Using a pastry brush, brush a 20 cm × 30 cm baking tray with a little olive oil, then sprinkle a little flour over the tray.

3 Sift the flour into a really big bowl. Sprinkle the dried yeast over the flour.

4 Make a well (a big hole) in the middle of the flour – you should be able to see the bottom of the bowl.

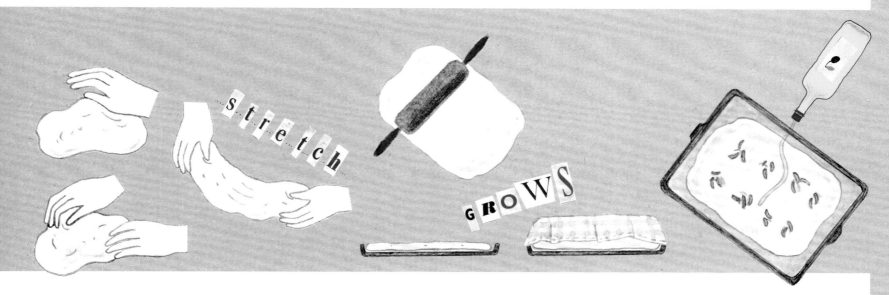

6 Sprinkle a little flour over the work surface and put the dough onto the flour. Knead the dough by pushing it away from you with the base of your hands and then pulling it back with your fingers. Do this for about 5 minutes until you can stretch the dough like a big piece of elastic. Using your hands and a rolling pin, stretch it into a rectangular shape, just a bit smaller than your baking tray, and put the dough into the tray. Cover with a slightly damp tea towel and leave in a warm place for about 1 hour, until it has doubled in size – watch it grow!

7 Turn the oven on to 220°C / 425°F / Gas Mark 7. Push your thumb into the dough all over to make dimples. Drizzle the oil over the top and sprinkle with the rosemary. Bake for 20–25 minutes until golden and cooked. Cut into rectangles, or tear it into pieces and share.

Marbled Ring Cake

This chocolate and vanilla cake is quite firm and not too sweet. It's great served for dessert with fruit, or you could pack a slice in your lunchbox as a snack. You could even try toasting and buttering a slice – it's delicious!

Makes enough for 6–8 people
- 100 g unsalted butter plus a little extra for greasing the cake tin
- 400 g self-raising flour
- 1 teaspoon baking powder
- 100 g golden caster sugar
- 2 free-range eggs
- a few drops vanilla extract
- 175 ml milk plus 1 tablespoon of milk
- 2 tablespoons cocoa powder
- cocoa powder or icing sugar to decorate

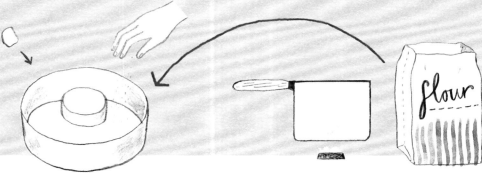
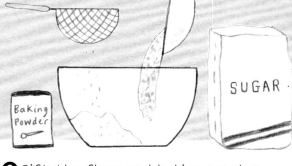

❶ Turn the oven on to 180°C/350°F/ Gas Mark 4. Grease a ring mould about 22 cm in diameter (or use a 20 cm round cake tin) – rub a little butter all over the inside. Sprinkle a little flour over the mould.

❷ Put the butter into a small saucepan and melt over a gentle heat or melt in a small bowl in the microwave. Leave to cool.

❸ Sift the flour and baking powder into a big bowl. Add the sugar.

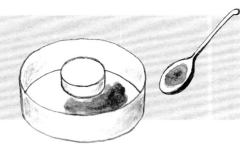

❼ Spoon the chocolate mixture into the greased mould. The cake mixture is quite stiff, so you will need to use two spoons to spoon it into the tin. Make sure it goes all the way round the tin!

❽ Spoon the vanilla cake mixture on top of the chocolate mixture. Whichever cake mixture you put into the tin first will come out on the top of the cake. If you want to create a really 'marbled' cake,

you can spoon alternate spoonfuls of each mixture into the tin, so that the finished cake has a swirly pattern instead of a layer of vanilla with a layer of chocolate on top of it.

4 Crack the eggs into a small bowl (see page 9). Add the cooled melted butter, milk and vanilla extract to the eggs and whisk together with a fork.

5 Pour the egg mixture into the bowl with the flour and carefully stir everything together.

6 Spoon half of the mixture into another bowl, add the cocoa powder and 1 tablespoon of milk and mix again.

9 Using oven gloves, put the cake in the oven and bake for 20 minutes. To see if it is cooked, poke a skewer or knife into the cake – it should come out clean. If there is sticky cake mixture on the skewer, put the cake back into the oven for 3–4 minutes. Put the cake tin on a cooling rack and leave for about 15 minutes. Carefully turn the tin upside down and take the cake out of the tin. Leave to cool.

10 Using a small sieve, sprinkle cocoa powder or icing sugar all over the cake to decorate.

Orange Cake

<u>Makes enough for 6–8 people</u>
For the cake:
- 100 g unsalted butter plus
  extra for greasing the cake tin
- 1 orange
- 2 free-range eggs
- 100 g golden caster sugar
- 100 g icing sugar
- 100 g self-raising flour
- ½ teaspoon baking powder

For the icing:
- 100 g icing sugar
- 1 orange

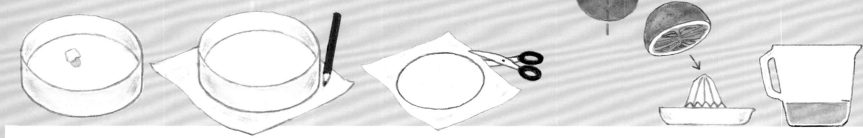

1 Turn the oven on to 180°C／350°F／Gas Mark 4. Grease a 20 cm cake tin – rub a little butter all over the inside.

2 Sit the tin on a piece of baking paper and draw around it, then cut out the circle and use it to line the bottom of the tin.

3 Using the bridge technique (see page 8), cut the orange in half and then squeeze the juice into a measuring jug. You need about 90 ml of juice, so if your orange is really juicy and has more juice than that, you could drink the rest.

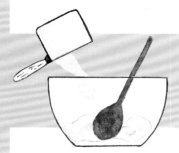

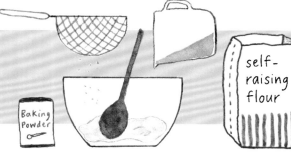

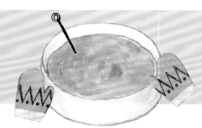

7 Stir in the cooled melted butter.

8 Sift the flour and baking powder onto the egg mixture, pour over the orange juice and carefully mix everything together. Pour the mixture into the cake tin.

9 Using oven gloves, put the cake in the oven and bake for 18 minutes. To see if it is cooked, poke a skewer or knife into the middle – it should come out clean. If there is sticky cake mixture on the skewer, put the cake back into the oven for 3–4 minutes.

This cake has an amazing orange flavour. It's quite a flat cake – it will rise in the oven, but it won't be big and tall.

4 Put the butter into a small saucepan and melt over a gentle heat or melt in a small bowl in the microwave. Leave to cool.

5 Crack the eggs into a big bowl (see page 9).

6 Add the golden caster sugar and icing sugar and using a whisk (either a hand whisk or electric whisk) whisk until light and fluffy.

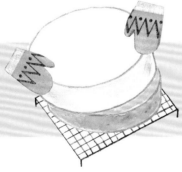

10 Using oven gloves, take the cake out of the oven. Leave to cool in the tin and then carefully turn the cake out onto a cooling rack so that it is the right way up.

11 Make the icing. Using the bridge technique, cut the orange in half and squeeze out the juice (see page 9). Sift the icing sugar into a bowl, add the orange juice and mix together.

12 Poke a few holes in the cooled cake with a skewer or a fork and then pour the icing over the top of the cake – it will run all over the cake into the holes, down the sides and onto the table!

Hazelnut Cake

This is a simple and delicious cake to make. The lemon zest (the grated yellow rind of a lemon) adds a wonderful flavour and the nuts give the cake texture. If you want the cake to taste even more lemony, you can mix the juice of the lemon with a little icing sugar and drizzle this over the cake.

Makes enough for 6–8 people
- 100 g unsalted butter plus extra for greasing the cake tin
- 200 g whole hazelnuts (or ground almonds, to save time)
- 200 g self-raising flour
- 200 g golden caster sugar
- 1 lemon
- 2 free-range eggs
- 50 ml milk
- icing sugar, for dusting the top of the cake

1 Turn the oven on to 180°C/350°F/Gas Mark 4. Grease a 20 cm cake tin – rub a little butter all over the inside.

2 Sit the tin on a piece of baking paper and draw around it, then cut out the circle and use it to line the bottom of the tin.

3 Put the butter into a small saucepan and melt over a gentle heat or melt in a small bowl in the microwave. Leave to cool.

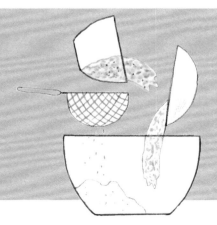 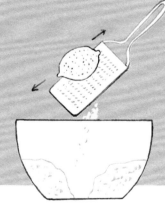 

6 Sift the flour into a big bowl. Add the sugar and ground nuts to the flour.

7 Grate the lemon zest (see page 9). Watch your fingers and keep them well away from the grater! Add the zest to the flour. Stir together and then make a well in the middle of the bowl so that you can see the bottom.

8 Crack the eggs into a jug (see page 9). Add the cooled melted butter and milk and mix with a fork.

WHIZZ

WhiRR

4 To make the hazelnuts taste even more nutty, you can 'toast' them in a frying pan over a gentle heat. It will only take a few minutes – you don't want them to be too brown. Move them around the pan with a wooden spoon so they don't burn.

5 Put the hazelnuts into a food processor and whizz until they are finely chopped. Ask an adult to help you with this (see page 7). If you don't have a food processor, you can put the nuts in a plastic bag and bash them with a rolling pin.

If you want to save time, you can use ground almonds instead of toasting and grinding whole hazelnuts.

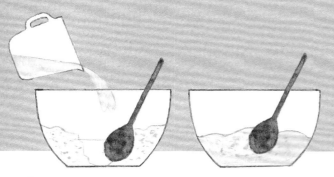

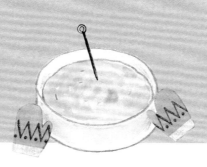

9 Pour the egg mixture into the well in the bowl and then carefully stir the egg mixture so that you gradually bring all the ingredients together.

10 Spoon the cake mixture into the tin. Using oven gloves, put in the oven and bake for 30 minutes. Test to see if the cake is cooked by poking a skewer into the middle. If the skewer comes out clean, the cake is cooked. If it has cake

mixture stuck to it, put the cake back into the oven for another 5 minutes. Leave to cool in the tin and then carefully turn the cake out onto a cooling rack. Using a small sieve, sprinkle icing sugar all over the cake to decorate.

Stuffed Peaches

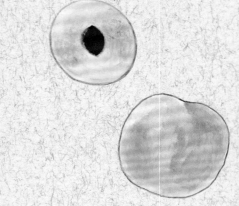

Makes enough for 4 people
- about 15 g unsalted butter
- 5 peaches
- 4 amaretti biscuits
- 2 free-range eggs
- 15 g cocoa powder
- 50 g golden caster sugar

Amaretti are small, dome-shaped Italian biscuits made with almonds. They're very light, with a crunchy texture. These stuffed peaches are good on their own, or served with ice cream or yogurt.

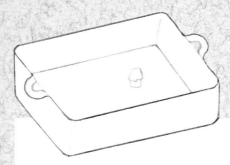

1 Turn the oven on 160°C / 325°F / Gas Mark 3. Rub a little butter all over an ovenproof dish (keep the remaining butter for later).

Twist

2 Using the bridge technique (see page 8) cut the peaches in half. Twist the peaches to help separate the halves.

3 Use a teaspoon to scoop out the stones. Using the claw technique (see page 8), cut one of the peaches into small pieces and put into a bowl.

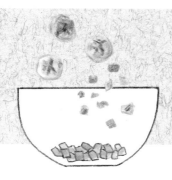

7 Using your hands crush the amaretti biscuits into small pieces and add to the chopped peach.

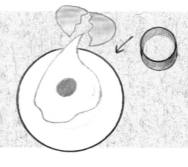

8 You need to separate the eggs as you only need the yolks (the orange part) for this recipe. Crack the egg (see page 9) onto a saucer. Then carefully put a small biscuit cutter over the yolk and tilt the

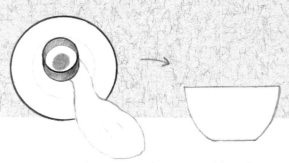

saucer to pour the egg white into a bowl, leaving the yolk inside the cutter on the saucer. Do the same with the other egg. Keep the egg whites to make meringues or add them to an omelette.

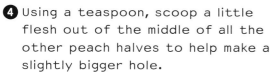
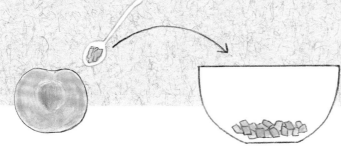

4 Using a teaspoon, scoop a little flesh out of the middle of all the other peach halves to help make a slightly bigger hole.

5 Put these bits of flesh into the bowl with the chopped peach.

6 Put the peach halves into the ovenproof dish with the cut side facing upwards.

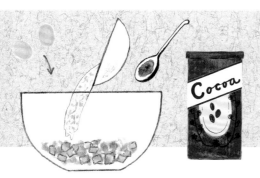
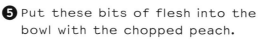

9 Add the egg yolks, cocoa powder and sugar to the crushed amaretti biscuits and mix everything together.

10 Divide the mixture among the peach halves – pile it up into a dome shape, and dot each one with a tiny bit of butter. Using oven gloves, put in the oven and bake for 1 hour. Serve hot or warm.

Banana Cream

To make this quick, easy and deliciously creamy dessert, you need really nice ripe bananas. This recipe makes a small amount of dessert for four people. You can always increase the quantities to make more!

Makes enough for 4 people
- 2 ripe bananas plus an extra banana to decorate (optional)
- ½ lemon
- 4 tablespoons mascarpone cheese
- 8 tablespoons natural yogurt
- 4 teaspoons runny honey
- pinch ground cinnamon

❶ Peel the bananas and put the flesh into a bowl. Using a potato masher or a fork mash the bananas until smooth. Squeeze the lemon juice over the bananas and mix with a fork.

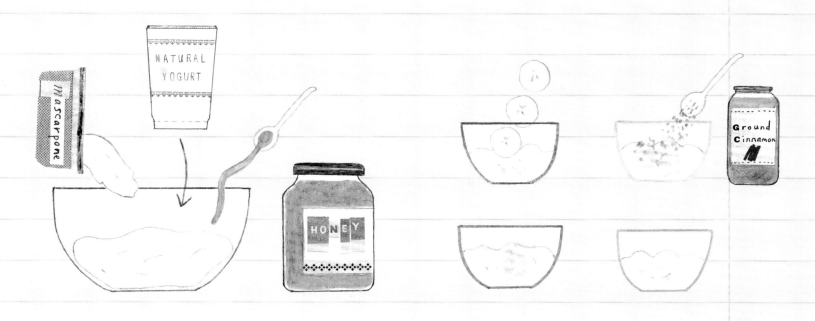

2 Add the mascarpone cheese and yogurt to the mashed banana and mix together, then swirl through the honey.

3 Spoon into small serving dishes. If you like, you can put a few slices of banana on top to decorate. Sprinkle with a little ground cinnamon and serve.

Fruits of the forest ice cream

You don't need an ice cream machine to make this berry ice cream, only a freezer. It's quick and simple, and an amazing colour.

Makes enough for 6–8 people
- 284 ml double cream
- 400 g frozen berries, such as blackberries, raspberries, redcurrants or blackcurrants (you will need a mixture of berries)
- ½ lemon
- 175 g golden caster sugar

❶ Pour the cream into a big bowl and using a hand whisk or electric whisk, whisk it until it holds in soft peaks – when you lift the whisk out of the cream, it should look like the picture of snowy mountains on the opposite page! If you whisk the cream for too long, it will become too firm and stiff.

❷ Put the frozen berries into a food processor. Squeeze the lemon juice over the fruit, add the sugar and whizz until the berries are mashed up. Ask an adult to help with the food processor (see page 7).

❸ Spoon the mashed fruit into the whipped cream and carefully fold everything together. Spoon into a freezeproof container (a clean used ice cream container or Tupperware pot is ideal) cover with a tight-fitting lid and freeze for 3 hours or until frozen.

WHISK

WHIZZ

Whir

Whi R

Whizz

Phaidon Press Limited
Regent's Wharf
All Saints Street
London N1 9PA

www.phaidon.com

First published 2009
© 2009 Phaidon Press Limited

The recipes in this book are adapted from
The Silver Spoon, © 2005 Phaidon Press Limited
which was first published in Italian in 1950,
eighth edition (revised, expanded and
redesigned 1997) © Editoriale Domus S.p.A.

ISBN 9 780 7148 5746 6 (UK edition)

A CIP catalogue record for this book
is available from the British Library.

Photographs by Angela Moore
Printed in China